Microwave Magic

Quick Meals

Grolier Limited
TORONTO

Contributors to this series:

Recipes and Technical Assistance:
École de cuisine Bachand-Bissonnette
Cooking consultants:
Denis Bissonette
Michèle Émond
Dietician:
Christiane Barbeau
Photos:
Laramée Morel Communications
Audio-Visuelles
Design:
Claudette Taillefer
Assistants:
Julie Deslauriers
Philippe O'Connor
Joan Pothier
Accessories:
Andrée Cournoyer
Writing:
Communications La Griffe Inc.
Text Consultants:
Cap et bc inc.
Advisors:
Roger Aubin
Joseph R. De Varennes
Gaston Lavoie
Kenneth H. Pearson

Assembly:
Carole Garon
Vital Lapalme
Jean-Pierre Larose
Carl Simmons
Gus Soriano
Marc Vallières
Production Managers:
Gilles Chamberland
Ernest Homewood
Production Assistants:
Martine Gingras
Catherine Gordon
Kathy Kishimoto
Peter Thomlison
Art Director:
Bernard Lamy
Editors:
Laurielle Ilacqua
Susan Marshall
Margaret Oliver
Robin Rivers
Lois Rock
Jocelyn Smyth
Donna Thomson
Dolores Williams
Development:
Le Groupe Polygone Éditeurs Inc.

We wish to thank the following firms, PIER I IMPORTS and LE CACHE
POT, for their contribution to the illustration of this set.

The series editors have taken every care to ensure that the information
given is accurate. However, no cookbook can guarantee the user successful
results. The editors cannot accept any responsibility for the results obtained
by following the recipes and recommendations given.

Canadian Cataloguing in Publication Data

Main entry under title:

Quick meals

(Microwave magic ; 14)
Translation of: Les Repas rapides.
Includes index.
ISBN 0-7172-2435-X

1. Microwave cookery.   I. Series: Microwave magic
(Toronto, Ont.) ; 14.

TX832.R4613 1988   641.5'882   C88-094213-4

Contents

Microwave Magic is a multi-volume set, with each volume devoted to a particular type of cooking. So, if you are looking for a chicken recipe, you simply go to one of the two volumes that deal with poultry. Each volume has its own index, and the final volume contains a general index to the complete set.

Microwave Magic puts over twelve hundred recipes at your fingertips. You will find it as useful as the microwave oven itself. Enjoy!

Note from the Editor

How to Use this Book
The books in this set have been designed to make your job as easy as possible. As a result, most of the recipes are set out in a standard way.

We suggest that you begin by consulting the information chart for the recipe you have chosen. You will find there all the information you need to decide if you are able to make it: preparation time, cost per serving, level of difficulty, number of calories per serving and other relevant details. Thus, if you have only 30 minutes in which to prepare the evening meal, you will quickly be able to tell which recipe is possible and suits your schedule.

The list of ingredients is always clearly separated from the main text. When space allows, the ingredients are shown together in a photograph so that you can make sure you have them all without rereading the list—

another way of saving your valuable time. In addition, for the more complex recipes we have supplied photographs of the key stages involved either in preparation or serving.

All the dishes in this book have been cooked in a 700 watt microwave oven. If your oven has a different wattage, consult the conversion chart that appears on the following page for cooking times in different types of oven. We would like to emphasize that the cooking times given in the book are a minimum. If a dish does not seem to be cooked enough, you may return it to the oven for a few more minutes. Also, the cooking time can vary according to your ingredients: their water and fat content, thickness, shape and even where they come from. We have therefore left a blank space on each recipe page in which you can note

the cooking time that suits you best. This will enable you to add a personal touch to the recipes that we suggest and to reproduce your best results every time.

Although we have put all the technical information together at the front of this book, we have inserted a number of boxed entries called **MICROTIPS** throughout to explain particular techniques. They are brief and simple, and will help you obtain successful results in your cooking.

With the very first recipe you try, you will discover just how simple microwave cooking can be and how often it depends on techniques you already use for cooking with a conventional oven. If cooking is a pleasure for you, as it is for us, it will be all the more so with a microwave oven. Now let's get on with the food.

The Editor

Key to the Symbols
For ease of reference, the following symbols have been used on the recipe information charts.

The pencil symbol ✏️ is a reminder to write your cooking time in the space provided.

Level of Difficulty

🍴 Easy

🍴🍴 Moderate

🍴🍴🍴 Complex

Cost per Serving

$ Inexpensive

$ $ Moderate

$ $ $ Expensive

Power Levels

All the recipes in this book have been tested in a 700 watt oven. As there are many microwave ovens on the market with different power levels, and as the names of these levels vary from one manufacturer to another, we have decided to give power levels as a percentage. To adapt the power levels given here, consult the chart opposite and the instruction manual for your oven.

Generally speaking, if you have a 500 watt or 600 watt oven you should increase cooking times by about 30% over those given, depending on the actual length of time required. The shorter the original cooking time, the greater the percentage by which it must be lengthened. The 30% figure is only an average. Consult the chart for detailed information on this topic.

Power Levels

HIGH: 100% - 90%	Vegetables (except boiled potatoes and carrots) Soup Sauce Fruits Browning ground beef Browning dish Popcorn
MEDIUM HIGH: 80% - 70%	Rapid defrosting of precooked dishes Muffins Some cakes Hot dogs
MEDIUM: 60% - 50%	Cooking tender meat Cakes Fish Seafood Eggs Reheating Boiled potatoes and carrots
MEDIUM LOW: 40%	Cooking less tender meat Simmering Melting chocolate
DEFROST: 30% **LOW: 30% - 20%**	Defrosting Simmering Cooking less tender meat
WARM: 10%	Keeping food warm Allowing yeast dough to rise

Cooking Time Conversion Chart

700 watts	600 watts*
5 s	11 s
15 s	20 s
30 s	40 s
45 s	1 min
1 min	1 min 20 s
2 min	2 min 40 s
3 min	4 min
4 min	5 min 20 s
5 min	6 min 40 s
6 min	8 min
7 min	9 min 20 s
8 min	10 min 40 s
9 min	12 min
10 min	13 min 30 s
20 min	26 min 40 s
30 min	40 min
40 min	53 min 40 s
50 min	66 min 40 s
1 h	1 h 20 min

* There is very little difference in cooking times between 500 watt ovens and 600 watt ovens.

Lucky People Who Know How To Manage Their Time

We all know people who never have the time to do everything they would like to do. Rarely are they able to manage both their jobs and their housework. House cleaning, dishes, shopping, meal preparation—all get neglected at one time or another. These people keep trying, but they always seem to be running around in circles, complaining that they have no free time. It is easy for many or us, busy ourselves, to sympathize with them.

On the other hand, we all also know people who are energetic and well organized. They have regular jobs, are able to look after their children and their homes, do their shopping in less time than most of us take and never seem to run short of anything. Aside from these everyday accomplishments, they manage to have some time for leisure activities.

They see the latest film, read the latest book and plan to attend that special concert next month. As if that isn't enough, these human dynamos also find the time to cook. Within half an hour they have dinner on the table, complete with a home-made dessert. And on top of that, they regularly cook for company too.

How do they do it? Is it temperament? Vitality? Or just plain luck? The key to this mystery is organization. These people are inclined to plan ahead, everything from holidays to shopping lists, and are thus able to handle their activities in a most efficient way. It doesn't take a genius to see the benefits of being organized and anyone can develop this attribute with a bit of time and patience.

This volume, *Quick Meals*, was designed to help you economize in terms of time spent on domestic chores. It will teach you all the steps you should follow to speed up meal preparation. You will learn how to plan your menus one week in advance, enabling you to shop more efficiently for them. You will also find many practical ideas for storing, freezing and defrosting various foods. You will learn how to prepare your meals more efficiently and make maximum use of your time in the kitchen. Finally, you will have a large file of recipes for nourishing, well-balanced and attractive meals which, for the most part, can be prepared in 30 minutes or less. Efficient use of your microwave oven makes all this possible.

You, too, will soon join the ranks of those active people who seem to find the time to do everything they wish to do. The lucky ones!

Efficient Meal Planning

You have a job and your obligations are many. As well, it is your responsibility to plan the menu for your family each day, to do the shopping and then to prepare the meals. You do manage to get it all done, but even the admiration of family and friends cannot always overcome your feelings that it is all too much for you.

You have no choice, however, and must do the best you can. It might therefore be necessary to take a good look at the way in which you organize your activities; poor planning is often the cause of frustration and stress. Even something as the preparation of the meals themselves in an efficient way.

Let's examine each of these five steps in greater detail. The best way to plan your menus is to draw up a chart of all the meals to be served over a one-week period. This approach will give you an overview of all these meals and provide an opportunity to balance your choices, taking into consideration your budget, your family's preferences and good nutrition.

A shopping list of the ingredients required to prepare these menus is then compiled. Knowing ahead of time the exact items needed and in what quantity enables you to make one shopping trip and to buy only what you need, thereby saving time and money.

Buying the ingredients needed for a period of one week no longer means worrying about their deterioration. On the contrary, with modern refrigeration methods as well as with the advent of the microwave oven, you can be assured that all the flavor and nutritional value will be preserved if the food is properly stored, whether it be refrigerated or frozen. Basic precautions are also essential to the proper defrosting of food in the microwave oven. With a little care, the quality of food that has been properly stored and defrosted will be surprising.

Everybody knows that preparing a meal does not simply mean putting it into

Menu Planning

the microwave oven. A good meal requires preparation of all the necessary ingredients in a certain order, and efficient preparation requires many steps and procedures. Time can be saved by using the proper tools and by cooking those items that require the longest cooking time first and using this time to prepare other items for cooking. You will find that this simple approach will save you several minutes a day and could well add up to hours over the course of one week. Using your small appliances, such as your electric mixer, blender and food processor can be helpful in your race against time. Making large quantities of certain preparations, such as soups, stews and sauces, which need only to be defrosted for another meal, will also save you additional time in the long run. This kind of detailed meal planning may be time-consuming in itself, but it is time well spent and the benefits include more leisure time for yourself—not to mention a more relaxed cook!

What can I cook for dinner today? How often have you asked this question, standing in front of your open cupboards, waiting for inspiration to strike? Sometimes, you sit at the kitchen table, desperately leafing through cookbooks, clippings or magazines. Some of the recipes would be fine but you don't have all the ingredients needed and you have no time to go shopping; other recipes are too similar to the meal you served just the other night. There is an ideal solution to this quandary but it is one that cannot be implemented ten or fifteen minutes before you must start dinner. If you had prepared your menus a week ahead and had done all the shopping required, there would be no need to rack

your brains this way. All the pitfalls making it necessary to improvise—indecision, inefficiency and repetition —could have been avoided. "An ideal solution," you say, "but who has the time to prepare menus for a whole week in advance?" You do. Remind yourself that you won't have to waste time every day deciding what to serve. It will all be done and, what is more, your list of menus can be used again whenever you wish. Convinced? Sit down, then, with pencil and paper and your favorite recipes. Take note of the following guidelines and say goodbye to those frustrating sessions of indecision that used to precede your meal preparation.

Prepare a Weekly Menu Chart

Use the chart on the right to draw up your own weekly dinner menu plan. You will find it very useful to see at a glance all the meals planned for the week. You may want to make changes after experimenting, so leave the chart in rough copy until you're sure you have it just the way you want it.

Dinner Menus For One Week

Day	Appetizer	Main Course	Dessert
Sunday	Stuffed mushrooms caps	Italian fondue	Chocolate trifle
Monday	Cream of vegetable soup	Macaroni casserole	Apple crisp
Tuesday	Tomatoes stuffed with avocado	Pork and peppers	Cherry caramel ring
Wednesday	Avocado bisque	Chicken salad	Bananas with maple syrup
Thursday	Brussels sprouts and parsnips with garlic	Steak and onions	Fruit kebabs
Friday	Yellow beans with fine herbs	Shrimp in cream sauce	Peach delight
Saturday	Mushroom soup	Veal escallops	Maple fondue

Time—A Precious Commodity

When selecting recipes for your menus, don't forget that time is probably the element that is in shortest supply. Preparation and cooking times for each dish should not exceed the time at your disposal. If your meal consists of an appetizer, a main dish and a dessert, make sure that you can prepare one dish while another is cooking and that your side dishes can be cooked in about the same time as the main dish. In choosing your menus, the activities of your family and yourself should also be taken into account. It would be pointless to choose to cook a complicated meal on those days when you or other members of the family have little time and must eat on the run. And, on the other hand, a more elaborate meal might be much appreciated and surely more easily prepared on a weekend, for instance.

Nutrition is of Prime Importance

One cannot repeat often enough that quick meals must not sacrifice good nutrition. Your menus should be well balanced and should follow established guidelines to make sure they contain all the ingredients necessary for good nutrition. Consult *Canada's Food Guide,* for example, for the quantities required daily by your family members of the foods outlined in its four major food groups.

As well, the nutritional quality of certain food products, such as many fruits and vegetables, is superior at certain times of the year—obviously, when they are in season. Try to take this fact into account when you are planning your weekly menus.

Variety is Important

Variety is an important consideration when making up your weekly menus. Having a large number of ingredients to choose from is preferable, in terms of nutritional value, to trying to use up a single item bought in quantity. Keeping your family's preferences in mind, you must choose different main dishes, side dishes and desserts for each day.

Keeping Within Your Budget

Planning meals ahead of time is also the best way to stay within your budget. A look at your menus will help you determine the cost of feeding your family for one week as well as the cost of each meal. You will then be able to decide when you can splurge a bit and when it is necessary to economize—without, however, sacrificing quality.

13

How To Organize Your Shopping

When making up your shopping list, be precise. The recipes you have chosen will dictate the ingredients you must buy or be sure you have on hand in sufficient quantity. You should know the exact amount of each ingredient needed for the entire week. While this may seem like a great deal of unnecessary calculating, remember that it will only have to be done once and that your shopping list can be used over and over again.

With such a list in hand, you need make only one trip to the supermarket, the fish market, the butcher's and so on. Having to go back for forgotten items is time wasted. Since you know what you need, you can also take advantage of the bargains advertised in the daily papers.

Before you go shopping, check your supplies to see what you need and in what quantity. This exercise will be less time-consuming than making an extra trip to the store. Don't wait until you run out before adding an item to your list—do it as soon as you notice your supply is running low. If you can't find the item at your usual store, you will then at least have time to locate it elsewhere and avoid last minute rushes.

One last bit of advice. Try to avoid shopping when the stores are crowded. Waiting in long lines is not good management of your time.

The following chart has been drawn up from all the recipes suggested in the section "Dinner Menus for One Week" (see pages 54 to 73). This chart clearly shows how detailed you can make your lists of required ingredients. Remember too—this is a permanent list, one that you can use as often as you wish.

Required Ingredients: Dinners for One Week

	Sun	Mon	Tues	Wed	Thurs	Fri	Sat	Total Amount
Milk Products								
Cream, 18%						500 mL	500 mL	1 L (4 cups)
Cream, 35%							50 mL	50 mL
Cheddar, grated	750 mL							750 mL (3 cups)
Emmenthal		125 mL						125 mL (1/2 cup)
Mozzarella, grated	250 mL	125 mL						375 mL (1-1/2 cups)
Yoghurt, plain				250 mL				250 mL (1 cup)
Meat, Fish, Seafood								
Beef, ground	225 g							225 g (1/2 lb)
Chicken				750 mL				750 mL (3 cups)
Pork tenderloin			675 g					675 g (1-1/2 lb)
Shrimp						450 g		450 g (1 lb)
Steak, round					675 g			675 g (1-1/2 lb)
Veal escallops							8	8
Fresh Fruit and Vegetables								
Alfalfa sprouts		375 mL						375 mL (1-1/2 cups)
Apples		1.25 L			1			900 g (2 lb)
Avocado			1	1/2				2
Bananas				4	1		1	6
Broccoli		250 mL		750 mL				1 large head
Brussels sprouts					450 g			450 g (1 lb)
Celery		250 mL	300 mL			125 mL		1 bunch
Green onions		8	30 mL				50 mL	10
Leeks							2	2

Required Ingredients: Dinners for One Week (continued)

	Sun	Mon	Tues	Wed	Thurs	Fri	Sat	Total Amount
Lettuce								1 head
Mushrooms	12 large					250 mL	250 mL	12 large 500 mL (2 cups)
Onions			30 mL		375 mL	1 + 125 mL		4
Oranges (fruit & zest)				15 mL		1		1
Parsnips			125 mL		250 mL			1
Peaches					1			1
Pears					1		1	2
Pecans			125 mL					125 mL (1/2 cup))
Peppers, green			2					2
Peppers, red			2			1	1	4
Pineapple	12 slices				1 slice		3 slices	2 pineapples
Tomatoes		3	4					7
Watercress						30 mL		30 mL (2 tablespoons)
Other Ingredients								
Beef broth					250 mL			250 mL (1 cup)
Beef consommé							284 mL	1 284 mL (10 oz can)
Breadcrumbs, Italian	60 mL							60 mL (4 tablespoons)
Buttermilk biscuits			284 g					284 g (10 oz)
Cake	12 slices							1 medium
Cake, sponge							1	1
Cereals, Special K		375 mL						375 mL (1-1/2 cups)
Cherries, green								4

Required Ingredients: Dinners for One Week (continued)

	Sun	Mon	Tues	Wed	Thurs	Fri	Sat	Total Amount
Cherries, maraschino			50 mL					50 mL (1/4 cup)
Cherries, red					4		20	24
Chicken broth			250 mL				50 mL	300 mL (1-1/4 cups)
Cream of asparagus soup		284 mL						1 284 mL (10 oz can)
Cream of tomato soup				284 mL			284 mL	2 284 mL (10 oz cans)
Maple syrup			30 mL	45 mL			125 mL	200 mL (7 oz)
Marmalade							15 mL	15 mL (1 tablespoon)
Orange juice					50 mL			50 mL (1/4 cup)
Pasta (spirals)		225 g						225 g (1/2 lb)
Peaches, canned						4 halves		1 540 mL (19 oz can)
Tomato ketchup					50 mL			50 mL (1/4 cup)
Tomato paste						30 mL		30 mL (2 tablespoons)
Tomato sauce, Italian	398 mL							1 398 mL (14 oz can)
Yellow beans						540 mL	540 mL	2 540 mL (19 oz cans)
Wine and Alcoholic Beverages								
Red wine	125 mL							125 mL (1/2 cup)
Sherry							50 mL	50 mL (1/4 cup)

Note that we have included only the main ingredients required for each recipe. Make sure you have a supply of the following basic items: butter, basil, brown sugar, cinnamon, cayenne, cocoa, cornstarch, cooking oil, eggs, flour, garlic, granulated sugar, honey, icing sugar, lemon juice, milk, nutmeg, oregano, paprika, pepper, parsley, sunflower seeds, salt, thyme and vanilla ice cream.

Storing Food

Having made up your menus and done your shopping, you have completed the first two steps in planning quick meals. The next step is very important—the proper storage of your purchases. Buying your food in advance is not enough; you want to serve it while it is at its peak in terms of flavor and nutritional value. To achieve this, you must keep certain basic principles in mind.

Food stored in the refrigerator should be hermetically sealed in order to protect it from the air. For items that will not keep more than a day or two, you will have to use your freezer.

Freezing is a simple process, one that anyone can use, but it should not be done without taking some precautions. Food to be frozen does require a certain amount of careful preparation before it is exposed to such low temperatures. The cold dry air, which preserves the food for long periods of time, can also cause it to deteriorate if not properly wrapped. You must, therefore, protect it by using a wrapping that is

airtight as well as watertight. Contact with the air can cause food to dry out and turn brown, a process known as freezer burn. You should also make sure that the wrapping, for meats especially, does not allow liquids either in or out, as they could contaminate other food in the freezer.

Containers, plastic bags and other wrappings that can be vacuum sealed may also be used for freezing. Rigid containers can be used as well but they should never be much larger than needed for the quantity of food being frozen. If there is too much air in the container, ice crystals form and the food will deteriorate more rapidly.

Regardless of the wrapping or the container used, you must always make sure that the package is hermetically sealed and is clearly labeled as to contents, quantity, date of freezing and maximum storage time. If the equipment for vacuum packing is unavailable, make sure you expel as much air as possible before sealing.

The plastic bags chosen for freezing should always be regular freezer bags and not those used by the supermarkets. Those used by the supermarkets are quite fragile and tear too easily in the freezer.

Since many dishes are safe in the microwave oven, it is possible to plan the freezing of your foodstuffs so that they can be put directly into the microwave for defrosting or cooking. Use round containers as often as possible to allow for more even distribution of the microwaves and therefore quicker and more uniform defrosting.

In order to make a well-sealed package that fits easily into the freezer, we recommend that you stack chops, steaks, fillets or patties. Putting a double thickness of plastic wrap between each one so that they are easy to separate, even before they're completely defrosted, will save you precious time.

A ring dish is ideal for freezing, defrosting and cooking ground beef. The energy of the microwaves is more concentrated toward the outside of the dish, and defrosting will therefore be more even because there is no meat in the center. This freezing method also applies to many cooked meat dishes, such as the all-purpose beef, pork and turkey preparations (pages 24, 26 and 28) that are used as bases in a number of the recipes for quick meals in this volume. If you package ground meat make a hole in the center before sealing the package for the freezer.

Different foods require different packaging. Chicken legs, for instance, should be separated with plastic wrap to speed up defrosting. Vegetables should be fresh and carefully washed. They will retain their color and flavor and will cook twice as quickly if they have been blanched. Vegetables should never be seasoned before freezing as the seasoning causes them to become dry and brittle. Fish should be scaled and cleaned and then, to prevent drying out, it should be surrounded with ice before being wrapped for the freezer.

Freezer Storage Times

Beef

Steaks	6 to 9 months
Stew beef	6 months
Ground beef	3 to 6 months
Cooked beef	3 months
Ground beef base (see page 24)	3 months

Lamb

Rib chops and cutlets	4 to 6 months
Loin chops	3 to 4 months
Cubes	3 to 4 months
Ground lamb	3 to 4 months
Cooked lamb	3 months

Pork

Chops	2 to 3 months
Cutlets	3 to 4 months
Ham slices	2 months
Ground pork	2 to 3 months
Pork base (see page 26)	3 months
Bacon	Not advisable

Pasta

Cooked, without sauce	2 to 3 months
Cooked, with meat sauce	1 to 2 months

Fish

Fatty fish	3 months
Partially fatty fish	4 months
Lean fish	6 months

Other Foods

	Foods
Rice, cooked	6 months

Poultry	
Turkey pieces	2 to 3 months
Turkey, boneless	4 to 5 months
Chicken pieces	4 to 5 months
Chicken, boneless	6 to 7 months
Turkey base (see page 28)	1 to 3 months
Cooked poultry	1 to 3 months

Veal	
Rib chops and cutlets	3 to 4 months
Loin chops	3 to 4 months
Cubes	3 to 4 months
Escallops	3 months
Ground veal	3 to 6 months
Cooked veal	3 months

Defrosting Food

Having put a great deal of effort into choosing the menus, buying the food and carefully storing the week's selections, you will of course want to take extra care during the defrosting process in order to preserve the full flavor and nutritional value of the food. Poor defrosting methods lead to a loss of quality, and there are some steps you can take to ensure good results.

You should make sure that meat or fish does not come into contact with any juice that collects during defrosting because liquids attract the microwaves and any meat standing in the juice would begin to cook. To avoid this problem, remove the meat from its wrapping and place it on a rack or on an upside-down saucer in a dish so that the meat does not come into contact with any juice that accumulates.

The weight of the food to be defrosted is important as this factor obviously determines the length of time necessary for proper defrosting. Using the accompanying chart, divide the total time required into two or three periods in the microwave with periods of standing time, equal to a quarter of the total defrosting time, in between.

And be sure to allow the same period of standing time at the end of the defrosting process. Remember, the molecules in the food remain active and the inside temperature continues to rise, even when removed from the oven. Therefore, the standing time is important for thorough and even defrosting.

A ring dish is ideal for defrosting because the energy of the microwaves is more concentrated toward the outside of the dish and defrosting will therefore be more even because there is no meat in the center. Meat patties, chops, escallops and fish fillets should be separated first and then arranged in a circle on a dish. If they have been frozen in a block, you will have to give them a short time in the microwave oven in order to separate them. Irregularly shaped pieces of meat should be placed on the dish with the thicker parts toward the outside and the thinner parts toward the inside.

Pieces of meat containing bone such as chops, steaks and poultry should be defrosted on a bacon rack or on a saucer placed upside down in the bottom of a dish, with the bony parts facing the center. Bones and liquids attract the microwaves and would cause uneven defrosting if they were facing the outside edge where the microwaves are strongest. Halfway through the defrosting process turn the meat over, leaving the bones facing the center. If some parts have defrosted, cover

them with aluminum foil before returning to the oven for the second defrosting cycle.

Food frozen in blocks, such as pasta and vegetables, should be separated as soon

as possible after a short defrosting cycle, and once more before the final defrosting cycle. Rearrange the food, moving the parts that have defrosted to the center and those that are still frozen to the outside edge.

Defrosting Guide

Food	Power	Defrosting Time
Lamb		
Rib chops and cutlets	30%	9 to 13 min/kg (4 to 6 min/lb)
Loin chops	30%	9 to 13 min/kg (4 to 6 min/lb)
Cubes	30%	9 to 13 min/kg (4 to 6 min/lb)
Ground lamb	30%	11 to 13 min/kg (5 to 6 min/lb)
Beef		
Steaks		
Large	30%	13 to 17 min/kg (6 to 8 min/lb)
Small	30%	11 to 13 min/kg (5 to 6 min/lb)
Cubes	30%	11 to 20 min/kg (5 to 9 min/lb)
Ground beef	30%	11 to 13 min/kg (5 to 6 min/lb)
Ground beef base		
(see page 24) 1/4 recipe	70%	5 to 6 min (stir twice)
Pork		
Chops	30%	7 to 13 min/kg (3 to 6 min/lb)
Cutlets	30%	7 to 13 min/kg (3 to 6 min/lb)
Ham slices	30%	7 to 13 min/kg (3 to 6 min/lb)
Ground pork	30%	11 to 13 min/kg (5 to 6 min/lb)
Pork base (see page 26)		
1/4 recipe	70%	8 to 10 min (stir twice)
Sausage	30%	7 to 9 min/kg (3 to 4 min/lb)
Veal		
Rib chops and cutlets	30%	7 to 13 min/kg (3 to 6 min/lb)
Loin chops	30%	7 to 13 min/kg (3 to 6 min/lb)
Cubes	30%	9 to 13 min/kg (4 to 6 min/lb)
Escallops	30%	7 to 13 min/kg (3 to 6 min/lb)
Ground veal	30%	11 to 13 min/kg (5 to 6 min/lb)

Defrosting Guide (continued)

Food	Power	Defrosting Time
Fish		
Fillets, in a block	30%	13 to 22 min/kg (6 to 10 min/lb)
Fillets, separated	30%	11 to 17 min/kg (5 to 8 min/lb)
Whole fish		
Small	30%	7-3/4 to 14-1/2 min/kg (3-1/2 to 6-1/2 min/lb)
Medium	30%	11 to 17-1/4 min/kg (5 to 8 min/lb)
Large	30%	13-1/2 to 22 min/kg (6 to 10 min/lb)
Pieces	30%	8-3/4 to 15-1/2 min/kg (4 to 7 min/lb)
Pasta		
Cooked, without sauce		
1 portion	70%	3 min
2 portions	70%	5 min
3 portions	70%	7 min
Cooked, with meat sauce		
1 portion	70%	4 min
2 portions	70%	6 min
3 portions	70%	8 min
Poultry		
Turkey breast, boneless	30%	11 to 13 min/kg (5 to 6 min/lb)
Chicken legs		
4 x 115 g (4 oz)	30%	8 min
8 x 115 g (4 oz)	30%	15 min
Chicken breast, boneless		
2 x 225 g (8 oz)	30%	8 min
4 x 225 g (8 oz)	30%	15 min
Turkey base (see page 28)		
1/4 recipe	70%	7 to 9 min (stir twice)
Other Foods		
Rice, cooked		
125 mL (1/2 cup)	70%	2 to 3 min
250 mL (1 cup)	70%	4 to 8 min

The time in the microwave must be alternated with standing times equal to a quarter of the total defrosting time. Divide the total defrost time into two or three periods in the microwave with the required periods of standing time in between, and let stand for the same period at the end of the defrosting cycle.

When whole fish is being defrosted, the head and tail should be covered with foil to prevent them from drying out and becoming brittle.

Finally, never forget that the final standing time is a very important step in the defrosting cycle.

We have included in this chart on freezer storage times only those foodstuffs that can be defrosted quickly. Large items such as hams or roasts have no place in the category of quick meals, the subject of this volume. Foods frozen in smaller quantities have a slightly shorter freezer life than those in larger quantities but, on the other hand, they do have the advantage of thawing more quickly. For efficient meal planning, you will have to keep this fact in mind when deciding whether it is to your advantage to freeze a particular food in large quantities or in individual portions.

Efficient Meal Preparation

Speed and efficiency in meal preparation should not preclude excellent quality or good nutrition. One of the best ways to save time is to prepare recipes that use "base" ingredients, which have been prepared and cooked in advance and then frozen. You will find such recipes on pages 24 to 29 in this volume and they can be used in many different ways. But there are many other foods that can be prepared and cooked in advance as well. Vegetables can be washed, cut, blanched and frozen; several kinds of soups freeze well; and certain sauces can either be refrigerated or frozen.

If you look at meal preparation as involving a series of steps and operations as well as the actual cooking, you can see that each operation might take a great deal of time when performed individually. But it is always possible to reduce that time by arranging these operations so that they overlap. Efficient meal preparation begins with the elimination of waiting periods, which are a waste of time. Organize the steps in your preparation in such a way as to have two operations going at the same time. If certain items take a long time to prepare, involving peeling, chopping, grating or mixing, for example, have something else in the process of cooking while you attend to these chores. Remember, you should always start with items that take the longest to cook. Once they have started to cook, you have time to prepare other items that take less time. Furthermore, those items that take the most cooking time, retain their heat longer than others and only need to be covered to remain hot.

Cooking Times for Frozen Vegetables*

Vegetable	Quantity	Cooking Time (at 100%)
Asparagus	284 g (10 oz)	3 to 5 minutes
Beans	284 g (10 oz)	4 to 5 minutes
Broccoli	284 g (10 oz)	3 to 5 minutes
Brussels sprouts	284 g (10 oz)	5 to 6 minutes
Carrots, sliced	284 g (10 oz)	5 to 6 minutes
Cauliflower, flowerets	284 g (10 oz)	5 to 6 minutes
Spinach	284 g (10 oz)	3 to 4 minutes
Summer squash, cubes	284 g (10 oz)	5 to 6 minutes
Corn, kernels	284 g (10 oz)	4 to 5 minutes
Corn, 1 cob		2 to 4 minutes
Each additional cob		1 to 2 minutes

* The cooking times in the above chart are for vegetables that have not been blanched before freezing.

Recipes Using All-Purpose Ground Beef Base

When you're in a hurry, any little trick that will save you a minute or two is appreciated. One time-saving trick is to cook up, in advance, large quantities of a particular item that may often be required in recipes. A good example is the following recipe, using lean ground beef, which we simply call our "all-purpose ground beef base."

Ingredients
1.8 kg (4 lb) lean ground beef
45 mL (3 tablespoons) cooking oil
4 onions, finely chopped
1 284 mL (10 oz) bottle chili sauce
1 package onion soup mix
1 package brown gravy mix

Method
— Cook the onions in the oil at 100% for 3 to 4 minutes; stir once during the cooking time.
— Add the ground beef and cook for 12 to 15 minutes at 100%; stir and break up the meat with a fork every 5 minutes.
— Add the remaining ingredients and mix well.
— Cover and cook at 100% for 4 to 6 minutes, stirring every 2 minutes.
— Allow to cool and freeze in four equal portions.

This ground beef base provides the meat for four meals. It may be kept in the refrigerator but it freezes very well and does not lose its flavor in the process. The ingredients have been selected to give it the greatest versatility possible. The four recipes suggested on the following page are only a partial list of ways to use this ground beef base. You will find it easy to adapt these recipes as well as to invent new ones, using this base as the main ingredient.

Curried Beef

Curry powder is one of the seasonings that will best enhance the flavor of your beef dishes. You can prepare a delicious and original meal by adding long grain rice, chopped green onions, chopped green pepper, brown gravy prepared from a mix, curry, chunks of tomato and soy sauce. A pure delight!

(See pages 30-31)

Beef and Macaroni Casserole with Corn

This ground beef base blends very well with pasta. You can create a delicious main dish by adding tomatoes that are peeled and cut in half, oregano, chili powder, kernel corn and elbow macaroni. Your family and guests will ask for more!

(See page 32-33)

Chinese Beef Casserole

As if by magic, this same ground beef base can take you from Italy to the Orient. To give it a Chinese flavor, simply add defrosted green peas, finely chopped celery, cream of mushroom soup, a little milk, soy sauce, almonds and Chinese noodles. An exotic creation is guaranteed!

(See pages 34-35)

Pita Bread Snack—Greek Style

A new use for an old standby! The following typically Mediterranean flavor transforms your ground beef base into a delicious snack—Greek style. Add some shredded lettuce and some tomato and cucumber salad with a spicy, oregano-flavored oil and vinegar dressing to the ground beef base and use as a stuffing for pita bread. A sunny taste of the Greek islands!

(See pages 36-37)

Recipes Using All-Purpose Pork Base

The all-purpose pork base recipe that follows works in the same way as the ground beef base. You can prepare enough pork for four meals and save yourself several steps in the preparation of each meal. This is the best way to use your time in the kitchen to advantage. You save repetitious steps and you also cut down on dirty dishes! The pork base is a large recipe, using pork tenderloin cut into bite-size pieces and lightly seasoned.

Ingredients
1.8 kg (4 lb) pork tenderloin
3 onions, finely chopped
250 mL (1 cup) celery, finely chopped
15 mL (1 tablespoon) flour
1 package pork gravy mix
50 mL (1/4 cup) water
5 mL (1 teaspoon) soy sauce
1 bay leaf
3 cloves garlic, crushed
salt and pepper to taste

Method
— Cut the pork tenderloin into 1.5 cm (1/2 in) cubes.
— In a dish, place the meat, onions, celery and flour and mix well.
— Add all the other ingredients and mix well.
— Cook for 10 minutes at 100% and stir.
— Lower the power to 70% and cook for 15 to 25 minutes, or until the pork is tender. Stir twice during the cooking period.
— Allow to cool. Divide into four portions and freeze.

This pork base provides the meat for four meals. It may be kept in the refrigerator but it freezes very well and does not lose its flavor in the process. The seasonings have been selected to give it the greatest versatility possible.

The four recipes suggested on the following page are only a partial list of ways to use this pork base. You will find it easy to adapt these recipes as well as to invent new ones, using this base as the main ingredient.

Pork and Onions

This simple recipe really hits the spot! Three Spanish onions for flavor, cooked potatoes and beef broth thickened with cornstarch are all that is required with the pork base to produce a very quick and nutritious meal.
Also delicious!

(See pages 38-39)

Pork with Leeks

The distinctive flavor of the white part of the leeks, especially in season, enhances this recipe and transforms the pork base into an original, well-balanced dish. Add bacon slices, sliced whites of leeks, kernel corn, frozen lima beans and chicken broth for a surprisingly delicious treat.
Another favorite!

(See pages 40-41)

Pork with Fine Herbs

The aroma of a mixture of fine herbs helps to transform our pork base into yet another exotic creation. You need only to add chicken broth, diced carrots and potatoes, chopped garlic, thyme, sage, parsley and Dijon mustard. The first bite tells the tale!

(See pages 42-43)

Pork with Red Peppers

This pork base lends itself to more highly seasoned dishes as well. Add lemon juice, Worcestershire sauce, brown sugar, cayenne, paprika and stips of roasted red pepper to obtain an extraordinary dish.
No one will complain about humdrum food when you serve this dish!

(See pages 44-45)

Recipes Using All-Purpose Turkey Base

Where quick meals are concerned, poultry does not take a back seat to beef or pork. Poultry too can be prepared in advance in large quantities and then used as the prime ingredient in many recipes. The following recipe for an all-purpose turkey base will save a lot of time and will provide delicious and nutritious meals.

Ingredients
1.8 kg (4 lb) turkey breast, boned
50 mL (1/4 cup) flour
2 onions, finely chopped
30 mL (2 tablespoons) powdered chicken concentrate
15 mL (1 tablespoon) parsley
2 mL (1/2 teaspoon) basil
2 mL (1/2 teaspoon) marjoram
pepper to taste

Method
— Cut the turkey into cubes and sprinkle with the flour.
— Mix the floured turkey and all the other ingredients together in a dish.
— Cook at 90% for 10 to 15 minutes, or until the mixture is cooked, stirring twice during the cooking time.
— Allow to cool. Divide into four portions and freeze.

This turkey base provides the meat for four meals. It may be kept in the refrigerator but it freezes very well and does not lose its flavor in the process. The seasonings have been selected to give it the greatest versatility possible.

The four recipes suggested on the following page are only a partial list of ways to use this turkey base. You will find it easy to adapt these recipes as well as to invent new ones, using this base as the main ingredient.

Turkey Ring

Ingredients reminiscent of the holiday season and an elegant appearance characterize this dish, and very little time is required to prepare it. Add to the turkey base the following ingredients: chopped celery, eggs, cooked rice, soft bread crumbs, chopped roasted red pepper, chicken broth and some pepper. Cook in a tube pan. Beautiful to look at—delicious to eat!

(See pages 46-47)

Turkey Véronique

Creamed turkey sounds delicious, but add grapes and you have an extraordinary dish. Simply add butter, cornstarch, 18% cream and seedless green grapes to the turkey base.
Absolutely delicious!

(See pages 48-49)

Turkey-Stuffed Avocado

The turkey base can be transformed into a delicious filling for avocado halves. Mix it with almonds, butter, chopped green pepper, mayonnaise, lemon juice and pepper. Serve the avocado halves on a bed of lettuce.
Avocado and turkey—a rare combination!

(See pages 50-51)

Turkey and Cheese Casserole

An unexpected but delightful delicious combination of diced carrots, defrosted green peas, milk, cheddar cheese soup, melted butter, cheese cracker crumbs and, of course, the turkey base.
An unforgettable taste!

(See pages 52-53)

Curried Beef

Level of Difficulty	
Preparation Time	10 min
Cost per Serving	$
Number of Servings	4
Nutritional Value	551 calories 31.8 g protein 6.6 mg iron
Food Exchanges	3 oz meat 2 vegetables exchanges 2 bread exchanges 1-1/2 fat exchanges
Cooking Time	25 min
Standing Time	None
Power Level	100%, 70%
Write Your Cooking Time Here	

Ingredients

1/4 recipe ground beef base, defrosted (see recipe, page 24)
250 mL (1 cup) long grain rice
500 mL (2 cups) hot water
5 green onions, chopped
1 green pepper, chopped
250 mL (1 cup) brown gravy, prepared from a mix
10 mL (2 teaspoons) curry
3 tomatoes, roughly chopped
15 mL (1 tablespoon) soy sauce
salt and pepper to taste

Method

— Place the rice and hot water in a covered dish and cook for 5 minutes at 100%. Reduce the power to 70% and cook for 10 minutes longer. Set aside.
— Place the onions and the green pepper in another dish; cover and cook at 100% for 4 minutes, stirring once.
— Add the beef base, gravy, curry, tomatoes, soy sauce and the cooked rice.
— Mix well and cook at 100% for 4 to 6 minutes, stirring once.
— Season to taste before serving.

This succulent recipe requires very little time and a minimum of preparation.

MICROTIPS

Blanching Vegetables Successfully

Freeze vegetables when they are in season and at their peak of freshness. You will get best results by blanching them before freezing. You must choose those that are the most fresh and wash them carefully. Do not season beforehand, as salt and certain other spices will affect their color and texture and frequently cause dehydration. Vegetables that have been blanched can be seasoned as they cook; they will then retain their natural color, flavor and crispness.

Beef and Macaroni Casserole with Corn

Level of Difficulty	🍴
Preparation Time	10 min
Cost per Serving	**$**
Number of Servings	4
Nutritional Value	576 calories 36.1 g protein 6.3 mg iron
Food Exchanges	3 oz meat 3 vegetable exchanges 1 fat exchange 2 bread exchanges
Cooking Time	16 min
Standing Time	None
Power Level	100%
Write Your Cooking Time Here	

Ingredients
1/4 recipe ground beef base, defrosted (see recipe, page 24)
250 mL (1 cup) elbow macaroni
1.5 L (6 cups) boiling water
1 540 mL (19 oz) can tomatoes, cut in half
5 mL (1 teaspoon) oregano
15 mL (1 tablespoon) chili powder
500 (2 cups) kernel corn, drained

Method
— Put the elbow macaroni and boiling water in a dish and cook, uncovered, for 5 to 7 minutes at 100%. Stir twice during the cooking.
— Drain the cooked macaroni and rinse in cold water. Set aside.
— Combine the remaining ingredients; mix well and add to the cooked macaroni.
— Cook at 100% for 7 to 9 minutes, stirring twice during the cooking time.

Chinese Beef Casserole

Level of Difficulty	⑪⑪
Preparation Time	15 min
Cost per Serving	$
Number of Servings	4
Nutritional Value	581 calories 40.6 g protein 7.5 mg iron
Food Exchanges	3 oz meat 3 vegetable exchanges 1 bread exchange 1/2 milk exchange 2 fat exchanges
Cooking Time	14 min
Standing Time	None
Power Level	100%
Write Your Cooking Time Here	

Ingredients
1/4 recipe ground beef base, defrosted (see recipe, page 24)
1 284 g (10 oz) package green peas, defrosted
500 mL (2 cups) celery, finely chopped
1 284 mL (10 oz) can cream of mushroom soup
30 mL (2 tablespoons) milk
15 mL (1 tablespoon) soy sauce
175 mL (3/4 cup) almonds, slivered
125 mL (1/2 cup) Chinese noodles

Method
— Place the beef base in a casserole and cook at 100% for 3 to 4 minutes.
— Distribute the green peas over the beef and add the chopped celery.
— In a bowl, mix the mushroom soup, milk and soy sauce and pour over the meat and vegetables.
— Top with the almonds, cover and cook at 100% for 7 to 10 minutes, or until the mixture is hot. Give the dish a half-turn halfway through the cooking time.
— Garnish with the Chinese noodles before serving.

One quarter recipe of the ground beef base plus a few nutritious ingredients are the basis for this remarkable dish.

Distribute the peas uniformly over the ground beef and then add the celery.

Pour the mixture of mushroom soup, milk and soy sauce over the assembled dish and add the almonds before cooking.

Pita Bread Snack—
Greek Style

Level of Difficulty	
Preparation Time	10 min
Cost per Serving	$
Number of Servings	4
Nutritional Value	306 calories 31 g protein 2.4 mg iron
Food Exchanges	3 oz meat 2 vegetable exchanges 1 bread exchange 2 fat exchanges
Cooking Time	5 min
Standing Time	None
Power Level	100%, 50%
Write Your Cooking Time Here	

Ingredients

1/4 recipe ground beef base, defrosted (see recipe, page 24)
30 mL (2 tablespoons) oil
15 mL (1 tablespoon) vinegar
15 mL (1 tablespoon) parsley
5 mL (1 teaspoon) oregano
1 small cucumber, unpeeled and chopped
1 tomato, chopped
250 mL (1 cup) lettuce, shredded
2 rounds of pita bread

Method

— Heat the ground beef base at 100% for 3 to 4 minutes, stirring once during the cooking time.
— In a bowl, mix the oil, vinegar, parsley and oregano. Add the cucumber and tomato to the dressing and mix well.
— Combine the meat, cucumber and tomato mixture and the shredded lettuce and mix well.
— Cut each pita round in half.
— Warm the pita halves at 50% for 1 minute.
— Stuff each pita half with a quarter of the cooked meat, cucumber, tomato and lettuce mixture and serve.

Tasty ingredients combine flavor and freshness to produce this popular snack.

Cut the pita bread in half; warm in the oven for 1 minute at 50%.

Stuff each pita half with the meat, cucumber, tomato and lettuce mixture.

MICROTIPS

To Defrost Half of a Package of Vegetables
Wrap half of the package in aluminum foil and place in the microwave oven for the first defrosting cycle.
Remove the partially thawed vegetables from the package, discard the foil, reseal the package and return to the freezer. Finish defrosting the partially thawed vegetables in a container.

Pork and Onions

Level of Difficulty	⑆
Preparation Time	15 min
Cost per Serving	$
Number of Servings	4
Nutritional Value	324 calories 31.8 g protein 5.6 mg iron
Food Exchanges	3 oz meat 2 vegetable exchanges 1/2 bread exchange
Cooking Time	13 min
Standing Time	None
Power Level	100%
Write Your Cooking Time Here	

Ingredients
1/4 recipe pork base, defrosted (see recipe, page 26)
3 Spanish onions, thinly sliced
1 540 (19 oz) can potatoes
150 mL (5 oz) beef consommé
15 mL (1 tablespoon) cornstarch
30 mL (2 tablespoons) cold water

Method
— Place the onion slices in a dish; cover and cook for 4 to 5 minutes at 100%.
— Add the pork base and potatoes to the onions and mix well. Set aside.
— Place the consommé in a dish; dissolve the cornstarch in the cold water, add to the consommé and cook for 2 to 3 minutes at 100%.
— Add this sauce to the meat mixture and cook at 100% for 4 to 5 minutes, stirring once during the cooking time.

MICROTIPS

Freezing Pasta

Now you can freeze leftover pasta because the microwave is ideal for defrosting and reheating it so that it will not be too soggy or too dry. It is very important, however, to protect the pasta from the cold, dry air of the freezer. You should therefore choose containers that have a good seal; they should not be covered with plastic wrap alone. To save yourself some time, choose round containers for even defrosting and make sure that they can safely go directly from the freezer to the microwave oven.

Another way to freeze pasta is to divide the leftovers into individual portions and place them in freezer bags, making sure to expel the air before sealing the bags. When you want to defrost and heat the pasta, divide the defrosting time into two or three periods, remembering that the standing times in between and at the end of the cycle should equal a quarter of the total defrosting time. Use the standing times to stir the pasta.

Pork with Leeks

Level of Difficulty	
Preparation Time	15 min
Cost per Serving	$
Number of Servings	4
Nutritional Value	419 calories 37.5 g protein 6.7 mg iron
Food Exchanges	4 oz meat 1 bread exchange 1 fat exchange
Cooking Time	23 min
Standing Time	None
Power Level	100%
Write Your Cooking Time Here	

Ingredients
1/4 recipe pork base, defrosted (see recipe, page 26)
6 slices bacon
4 leeks, white only, thinly sliced
50 mL (1/4 cup) water
375 mL (1-1/2 cups) kernel corn, drained
250 mL (1 cup) frozen lima beans
125 mL (1/2 cup) chicken broth

Method
— Place the bacon slices on a rack and cover with paper towel to avoid spattering; cook at 100% for 5 to 7 minutes, or until crisp. Give the rack a half-turn halfway through the cooking time. Set aside.
— Place the sliced leeks in a dish with the water; cover and cook for 3 to 4 minutes at 100%. Stir once during the cooking time.
— Add the corn, lima beans, chicken broth and the pork base to the leeks. Mix well.
— Cover and cook the mixture at 100% for 10 to 12 minutes, stirring twice during the cooking time.
— Crumble the bacon and sprinkle over the mixture before serving.

The very ordinary ingredients assembled here make up a surprisingly tasty dish.

To cook the bacon, place it on a rack and cover with paper towel.

Put the sliced leeks in a dish and add the water. Cook for 3 to 4 minutes at 100%.

41

Pork with Fine Herbs

Level of Difficulty	(icon)
Preparation Time	20 min
Cost per Serving	$
Number of Servings	4
Nutritional Value	302 calories 30.1 g protein 5.2 mg iron
Food Exchanges	3 oz meat 1 vegetable exchange 1 bread exchange
Cooking Time	13 min
Standing Time	None
Power Level	100%
Write Your Cooking Time Here	(icon)

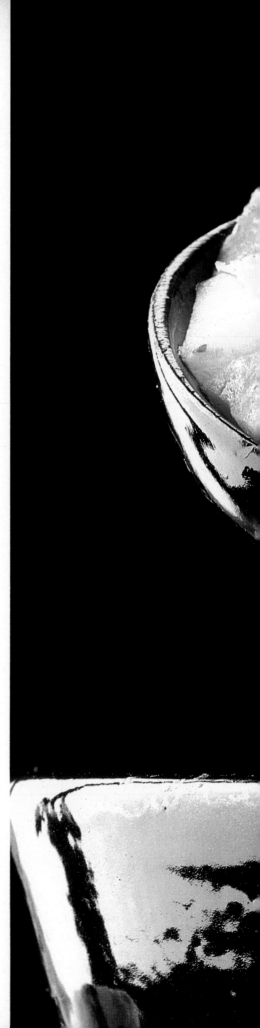

Ingredients
1/4 recipe pork base, defrosted (see recipe, page 26)
50 mL (1/4 cup) chicken broth
4 carrots, cut into cubes
4 potatoes, cut into cubes
2 cloves garlic, crushed
5 mL (1 teaspoon) thyme
2 mL (1/2 teaspoon) sage
5 mL (1 teaspoon) parsley
15 mL (1 tablespoon) Dijon mustard

Method
— In a large dish, combine all the ingredients except the pork base and mix well.
— Cook at 100% for 7 to 9 minutes or until the vegetables are tender, stirring once during the cooking time.
— Add the pork base, mix well and cook at 100% for 3 to 4 minutes.

Pork with Red Peppers

Level of Difficulty	
Preparation Time	15 min
Cost per Serving	$
Number of Servings	4
Nutritional Value	224 calories 27.2 g protein 4.5 mg iron
Food Exchanges	3 oz meat 1 vegetable exchanges
Cooking Time	9 min
Standing Time	2 min
Power Level	100%, 70%
Write Your Cooking Time Here	

Ingredients
1/4 recipe pork base, defrosted (see recipe, page 26)
45 mL (3 tablespoons) lemon juice
30 mL (2 tablespoons) Worcestershire sauce
15 mL (1 tablespoon) brown sugar
pinch cayenne pepper
2 mL (1/2 teaspoon) paprika
125 mL (1/2 cup) red pepper, roasted and cut into strips

Method
— In a dish, combine the lemon juice, Worcestershire sauce, brown sugar, cayenne and paprika; mix well and cook for 1 minute at 100%.
— Add the pork base and the red pepper strips and mix well.
— Reduce the power to 70% and cook the mixture for 6 to 8 minutes, stirring once during the cooking time.
— Let stand for 2 minutes before serving.

These very strongly flavored ingredients blend well with the pork base for a delicious meal.

MICROTIPS

To Defrost Fruit in Cartons

If the carton containing the fruit is made entirely of cardboard, you need only to open it and place it in a bowl to defrost its contents. If the carton has metal ends, however, stand it up in the oven—but remove the exposed metal end. Use 100% power and divide the defrosting cycle into several short periods. Try 2 minutes for a 284 mL (10 oz) carton and 2 to 3 minutes for a 455 mL (16 oz) carton.

Hard-Boiled Eggs without Dark Rings

Sometimes when you slice hard-boiled eggs, you find the yolks circled with dark rings. This spoils the appearance of the eggs and is especially annoying when you want to use them as a garnish. The rings have nothing to do with the freshness of the eggs but rather with the way in which they were cooked. There are two points to remember when cooking hard-boiled eggs. First of all, be very precise about the cooking time and do not leave them in the hot water any longer than necessary. And second, they must be cooled immediately by plunging them into cold water as soon as they are cooked.

Turkey Ring

Level of Difficulty	(icon)
Preparation Time	15 min
Cost per Serving	$
Number of Servings	4
Nutritional Value	357 calories 36.8 g protein 3 mg iron
Food Exchanges	4 oz meat 1 bread exchange
Cooking Time	13 min
Standing Time	4 min
Power Level	100%, 70%
Write Your Cooking Time Here	(icon)

Ingredients
1/4 recipe turkey base, defrosted (see recipe, page 28)
75 mL (1/3 cup) celery, chopped
4 eggs
250 mL (1 cup) rice, cooked
500 mL (2 cups) soft breadcrumbs
50 mL (1/4 cup) red pepper, roasted and chopped
500 mL (2 cups) chicken broth
pepper to taste

Method
— Place the celery in a dish; cover and cook for 1 to 2 minutes at 100%.
— Beat the eggs, pour them over the celery and then add all the other ingredients; mix well.
— Pour the mixture into a tube pan and cook for 9 to 11 minutes at 70%; give the dish a half-turn halfway through the cooking time.
— Allow the dish to stand for 4 minutes before serving.

Gather all the ingredients needed to produce this succulent dish.

Add the beaten eggs to the cooked celery and then add all the other ingredients.

Mix the ingredients well; pour into a tube pan and cook.

MICROTIPS

To Speed Up the Cooking Times for Firm Vegetables

When time is short, cooking such vegetables as potatoes, carrots and turnips can be a problem. You can speed up the process simply by grating them before putting them in the microwave oven.

Turkey Véronique

Level of Difficulty	🍴
Preparation Time	10 min
Cost per Serving	**$**
Number of Servings	4
Nutritional Value	340 calories 27.9 g protein 1.4 mg iron
Food Exchanges	4 oz meat 1/2 fruit exchange 3 fat exchanges
Cooking Time	7 min
Standing Time	None
Power Level	100%, 90%
Write Your Cooking Time Here	

Ingredients
1/4 recipe turkey base, defrosted (see recipe, page 28)
30 mL (2 tablespoons) butter
30 mL (2 tablespoons) cornstarch
60 mL (4 tablespoons) cold water
250 mL (1 cup) 18% cream
250 mL (1 cup) seedless green grapes

Method
— Preheat a browning dish for 7 minutes at 100%; add the butter and heat for 30 seconds at 100%.
— Sear the turkey in the butter and set aside.
— Dissolve the cornstarch in the cold water and add to the cream; mix with the turkey.
— Reduce the power to 90% and cook the mixture for 3 to 5 minutes, stirring once during the cooking time.
— Add the green grapes and continue to cook at 90% for 2 minutes, stirring once during the cooking time.

48

This classic but simple recipe is sure to delight.

Using a browning dish, sear the turkey base in 30 mL (2 tablespoons) of butter.

MICROTIPS

Filling Containers with Narrow Necks

Containers with narrow necks such as salt and pepper shakers can be difficult to fill without a funnel. When necessary, you can make a temporary funnel by cutting the corner off an envelope and using it as a substitute.

Turkey-Stuffed Avocado

Level of Difficulty	🍴🍴
Preparation Time	20 min
Cost per Serving	**$**
Number of Servings	4
Nutritional Value	698 calories 31.9 g protein 3.3 mg iron
Food Exchanges	4.5 oz meat 4 vegetable exchanges 6 fat exchanges
Cooking Time	4 min
Standing Time	None
Power Level	100%
Write Your Cooking Time Here	✏️🍎

Ingredients
1/4 recipe turkey base, defrosted (see recipe, page 28)
125 mL (1/2 cup) slivered almonds
45 mL (3 tablespoons) butter
1 red pepper, chopped
1 green pepper, chopped
125 mL (1/2 cup) mayonnaise
2 avocadoes, cut in half, stones removed
30 mL (2 tablespoons) lemon juice
pepper to taste
4 lettuce leaves

Method
— Place the almonds and butter in a dish and cook at 100% for 3 to 4 minutes stirring once.
— Drain the almonds and set aside.
— Place the turkey in a bowl; add the chopped peppers and the mayonnaise and mix well.
— Scoop some of the flesh out of the avocado halves, leaving about 0.5 cm (1/4 in) of the flesh lining the skin.
— Dice the avocado that has been removed and add it to the turkey mixture.
— Sprinkle the entire surface of the avocado halves with lemon juice and fill the hollows with the turkey mixture.
— Add pepper to taste and garnish with the almonds.
— Serve each avocado half on a lettuce leaf.

50

Turkey and Cheese Casserole

Level of Difficulty	🍴
Preparation Time	20 min
Cost per Serving	$
Number of Servings	4
Nutritional Value	494 calories 37.3 g protein 3.9 mg iron
Food Exchanges	4 oz meat 2 fat exchanges 1 bread exchange 1/2 milk exchange
Cooking Time	27 min
Standing Time	3 min
Power Level	100%, 70%
Write Your Cooking Time Here	

Ingredients
1/4 recipe turkey base, defrosted (see recipe, page 28)
250 mL (1 cup) potatoes, diced
250 mL (1 cup) carrots, diced
50 mL (1/4 cup) water
250 mL (1 cup) frozen green peas
250 mL (1 cup) milk
1 284 (10 oz) can cheddar cheese soup
250 mL (1 cup) cheese cracker crumbs
45 mL (3 tablespoons) butter, melted

Method
— Place the potatoes, carrots and water in a dish; cover and cook 3 to 5 minutes at 100%.
— Add the peas and continue to cook for 2 minutes at 100%. Add the turkey base, mix well and set aside.
— Mix the milk with the cheddar cheese soup and pour over the turkey mixture.
— Mix the cracker crumbs with the melted butter and sprinkle over the surface of the turkey mixture.
— Reduce the power to 70% and cook for 18 to 20 minutes, giving the dish a half-turn halfway through the cooking time.
— Allow to stand for 3 minutes before serving.

All these varied ingredients blend beautifully to gave you a well-balanced dish.

Once the potatoes and carrots are cooked, add the peas and cook 2 minutes at 100%.

After combining the turkey with the vegetables, add the mixture of milk and cheddar cheese soup.

Dinner Menus for One Week

If you have taken the trouble to make up, in advance, the menus for an entire week's evening meals, you have an excellent planning tool. With such a chart in hand you can make sure that you stay within your budget while, at the same time, providing nourishing meals. Advance planning also permits you to cater to the tastes of each member of your family.

In the following pages we offer you an excellent model to follow—seven complete dinner menus, each consisting of an appetizer, a main course and a dessert. The combined preparation and cooking times for each of these meals is surprisingly short, none exceeding 40 minutes and most not more than 30.

Not only do we recommend our menus but we would suggest that you combine some elements of one with those in another or that you create new ones, ones that might better suit your family. We are positive that you will find these menus very useful and, by creating new ones, before long you will have menus for several weeks in hand.

Sunday
Stuffed mushroom caps
Italian fondue
Chocolate trifle

Monday
Cream of vegetable soup
Macaroni casserole
Apple crisp

Tuesday
Tomatoes stuffed with avocado
Pork and peppers
Cherry caramel ring

Wednesday
Avocado bisque
Chicken salad
Bananas with maple syrup

Thursday
Brussels sprouts and parsnips with garlic
Steak and onions
Fruit kebabs

Friday
Yellow beans with fine herbs
Shrimp in cream sauce
Peach delight

Saturday
Mushroom soup
Veal escallops
Maple fondue

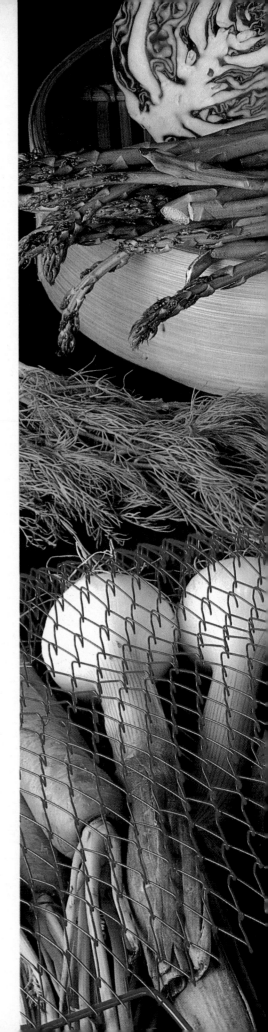

Sunday's Menu

Stuffed Mushroom Caps

Ingredients
12 large mushrooms
30 mL (2 tablespoons) butter
30 mL (2 tablespoons)
onions, finely chopped
50 mL (1/4 cup) Italian
breadcrumbs
parsley, chopped

Method
— Remove the mushroom
stems and chop finely; set
the mushroom caps aside.
— Put the butter, onion and
chopped stems in a dish.
Cook at 100% for 1 to
1-1/2 minutes, or until
tender.

— Add the breadcrumbs and
mix well.
— Stuff the mushroom caps
with this mixture and
cook at 100% for 1-1/2 to
2-1/2 minutes.
— Sprinkle with parsley
before serving.

Italian Fondue

Ingredients
225 g (8 oz) ground beef
1 398 mL (14 oz) can Italian
tomato sauce
750 mL (3 cups) cheddar
cheese, grated
250 mL (1 cup) mozzarella
cheese, grated
15 mL (1 tablespoon)
cornstarch
125 mL (1/2 cup) red wine
Italian bread, cut into cubes

Method
— Place the ground beef in a
dish and cook for 2 to 3
minutes at 100%; stir
halfway through the
cooking to break up the
meat.
— Add the tomato sauce and
cook for 2 to 3 minutes at
100%, stirring once
halfway through the
cooking time.
— Gradually add the grated
cheeses, stirring constantly
until melted. Set aside.

— Dissolve the cornstarch in
the red wine and add to
the mixture.
— Cook at 100% for 3 to 4
minutes or until the meat
sauce is slightly thickened.
— Pour the sauce into a
chafing dish or fondue
pot.
— Serve the fondue with
Italian bread cut into
cubes; dip the cubes into
the sauce with fondue
forks.

Chocolate Trifle

Ingredients
30 mL (2 tablespoons)
cornstarch
500 mL (2 cups) milk
45 mL (3 tablespoons) cocoa
125 mL (1/2 cup) sugar
12 slices of cake
12 slices of pineapple

Method
— Dissolve the cornstarch in
a small amount of the
milk and set aside.
— Pour the remaining milk
into a dish and add the
cocoa and sugar; cook at
100% for 4 minutes,
stirring once during the
cooking time.
— Add the dissolved

cornstarch and cook at
100% for 2 to 4 minutes,
stirring every minute.
— Place the cake slices in a
serving dish and cover
with the pineapple slices.
— Pour the sauce over the
pineapple slices and
garnish as desired before
serving.

Monday's Menu*

Cream of Vegetable Soup

Ingredients
250 mL (1 cup) broccoli flowerets, cut into pieces
250 mL (1 cup) celery, finely chopped
125 mL (1/2 cup) onion, finely chopped
50 mL (1/4 cup) water
1 284 mL (10 oz) can cream of asparagus soup
284 mL (10 oz) milk
1 mL (1/4 teaspoon) thyme

Method
— Put the broccoli, celery, onion and water into a dish; cover and cook at 100% for 4 to 5 minutes, stirring once.
— Drain the vegetables when cooked and set aside.
— In a bowl, mix the asparagus soup with the milk; add to the cooked vegetables and add the thyme.
— Cook the soup at 100% for 4 to 5 minutes, stirring once during the cooking time.

Macaroni Casserole

Ingredients
225 g (8 oz) spiral macaroni
1.5 L (6 cups) boiling water
45 mL (3 tablespoons) butter
8 green onions, chopped
45 mL (3 tablespoons) flour
500 mL (2 cups) milk
5 mL (1 teaspoon) dried basil
2 mL (1/2 teaspoon) thyme
2 mL (1/2 teaspoon) oregano
15 mL (1 tablespoon) parsley
salt and pepper to taste
125 mL (1/2 cup) Emmenthal cheese, grated
125 mL (1/2 cup) mozzarella cheese, grated
paprika to taste
3 tomatoes, quartered

Method
— Pour the boiling water into a dish and add the macaroni; cook at 100% for 7 to 9 minutes, or until cooked.
— Drain and rinse with cold water; set aside.
— In a dish, melt the butter and sauté the green onions for 2 minutes at 100%; add the flour and mix.
— Add the milk and cook for 5 to 7 minutes at 100%, beating with a whisk every 2 minutes.
— Add the basil, thyme, oregano, parsley, salt and pepper and mix well.
— Put the macaroni in a casserole dish and cover with the sauce; set aside.
— Combine the Emmenthal and mozzarella and spread over the macaroni and sauce.
— Sprinkle with paprika and cook for 5 to 6 minutes at 70%.
— Garnish with the tomato quarters before serving.

Apple Crisp

Ingredients
1.25 L (5 cups) apples, peeled and cut into large chunks
cinnamon to taste
nutmeg to taste
50 mL (1/4 cup) butter
250 mL (1 cup) Special K, coarsely crushed
125 mL (1/2 cup) dark brown sugar
15 mL (1 tablespoon) flour

Method
— Place the apple chunks in a dish and sprinkle with cinnamon and nutmeg.
— Melt the butter for 30 seconds at 100%.
— In a bowl, mix the cereal, brown sugar and flour. Add the melted butter and mix well.
— Spread this mixture over the apples and cook, uncovered, for 4 minutes at 100%.

* To save time, prepare the dishes in the following order: macaroni casserole, cream of vegetable soup and then the apple crisp.

Tuesday's Menu*

Tomatoes Stuffed with Avocado

Ingredients
4 tomatoes
30 mL (2 tablespoons) green onion, chopped
1 small avocado, peeled and diced
15 mL (1 tablespoon) lemon juice
15 mL (1 tablespoon) oil
pinch cayenne pepper
salt and pepper to taste
375 mL (1-1/2 cups) alfalfa sprouts

Method
— Slice 1.5 cm (1/2 in) off the top of each tomato.
— Remove the pulp.
— In a bowl, mix the tomato pulp, green onions, avocado, lemon juice, oil and cayenne. Season to taste and mix well.
— Add the alfalfa sprouts and mix lightly.
— Stuff the tomatoes with the mixture.

Cherry Caramel Ring**

Ingredients
50 mL (1/4 cup) butter
125 mL (1/4 cup) brown sugar, packed
30 mL (2 tablespoons) corn syrup or maple syrup
125 mL (1/2 cup) pecan halves
50 mL (1/4 cup) maraschino cherries, cut into quarters
1 284 (10 oz) package refrigerated buttermilk biscuits, uncooked

Method
— Put the butter in a 20 cm (8 inch) ring dish and cook for 1 minute at 100%.
— Add the brown sugar and syrup and mix well with a fork.
— Place the pecans and cherries in the bottom of the dish.
— Form a ring with the uncooked buttermilk biscuits.
— Cook, uncovered, for 6 to 8 minutes at 70%.
— Invert the pan onto a serving platter, allow the syrup to drizzle over the ring and serve warm.

Pork and Peppers

Ingredients
675 g (1-1/2 lb) pork tenderloin, cut into strips
15 mL (1 tablespoon) oil
1 clove garlic, crushed
2 green peppers, cut into strips
2 red peppers, cut into strips
30 mL (2 tablespoons) butter
30 mL (2 tablespoons) flour
250 mL (1 cup) chicken broth
15 mL (1 tablespoon) parsley, chopped
salt and pepper to taste

Method
— Preheat a browning dish for 7 minutes at 100% and add the oil.
— Sear the pork strips and the garlic; add the peppers and cook for 3 to 4 minutes at 100%; set aside.
— In a dish, melt the butter for 30 seconds at 100%, add the flour and mix.
— Add the chicken broth and cook at 100% for 3 to 4 minutes, stirring twice during the cooking time.
— Pour this sauce over the pork and pepper strips, sprinkle with parsley and season to taste.
— Cook the mixture at 100% for 3 to 4 minutes, stirring once.
— Allow to stand for 2 minutes before serving.

* To save time, prepare the dishes in the following order: the pork and peppers, the stuffed tomatoes and then the cherry caramel ring.

** Prepare all the ingredients for the cherry caramel ring beforehand and cook while serving the main course.

Wednesday's Menu*

Avocado Bisque

Ingredients
50 mL (1/4 cup) celery, chopped
250 mL (1 cup) milk
1 284 (10 oz) can cream of tomato soup
1/2 avocado, peeled and diced
15 mL (1 tablespoon) lemon juice

Method
— Place the celery in a dish; cover and cook for 2 to 3 minutes at 100%.
— While the celery is cooking, mix the milk with the tomato soup.
— Add the milk and soup mixture to the celery and cook at 100% for 4 to 6 minutes, stirring once.
— Add the diced avocado and cook at 100% for 2 to 3 minutes, stirring once.
— Add the lemon juice just before serving.

Chicken Salad

Ingredients
750 mL (3 cups) chicken, cooked and diced
750 mL (3 cups) broccoli flowerets
45 mL (3 tablespoons) water
250 mL (1 cup) celery, chopped
1 head of lettuce
50 mL (1/4 cup) sunflower seeds

Dressing
250 mL (1 cup) plain yoghurt
30 mL (2 tablespoons) honey
15 mL (1 tablespoon) orange zest

Method
— Peel the bananas and cut them in half lengthwise.
— Melt the butter in a dish for 30 seconds at 100%.
— Drain the broccoli and rinse under cold water. Set aside.
— Prepare the salad dressing by mixing the yoghurt, honey and orange zest; whip to a uniform consistency.
— In a bowl, mix the broccoli, chicken and celery.
— Arrange the lettuce leaves on a serving dish and spoon the chicken mixture onto them.
— Pour the dressing over the chicken mixture and sprinkle with the sunflower seeds before serving.

Bananas with Maple Syrup

Ingredients
4 bananas
30 mL (2 tablespoons) butter
45 mL (3 tablespoons) maple syrup
20 mL (4 teaspoons) lemon juice
15 mL (1 tablespoon) icing sugar

Method
— Pell the bananas and cut them in half lengthwise.
— Melt the butter in a dish for 30 seconds at 100%.
— Add the maple syrup and mix well.
— Place the bananas in a dish and spoon the syrup over them, making sure they are completely covered.
— Cook the bananas at 100% for 2 to 3 minutes, giving the dish a half-turn halfway through the cooking time.
— Sprinkle the bananas with the lemon juice and icing sugar before serving.

* To save time, proceed in the following way: cook the broccoli for the chicken salad, prepare the avocado bisque, prepare the salad and then cook the bananas with the maple syrup.

Thursday's Menu*

Brussels Sprouts and Parsnips with Garlic

Ingredients
450 g (1 lb) Brussels sprouts
250 mL (1 cup) parsnips, cut
in julienne strips
75 mL (1/3 cup) water
15 mL (1 tablespoon) garlic
butter
salt and pepper to taste

Method
— Place the Brussels sprouts
and parsnips in a dish
with the water; cover and
cook for 8 to 12 minutes
at 100%.
— Drain the vegetables and
set aside.

— Melt the garlic butter for
30 seconds at 100%.
— Add the garlic butter to
the vegetables.
— Season before serving.

Steak and Onions

Ingredients
675 g (1-1/2 lb) round steak,
cut into strips
30 mL (2 tablespoons) butter
15 mL (1 tablespoon) oil
375 mL (1-1/2 cups) onions,
thinly sliced
15 mL (1 tablespoon)
cornstarch
45 mL (3 tablespoons) water
250 mL (1 cup) beef broth
50 mL (1/4 cup) ketchup
5 mL (1 teaspoon) sugar
salt and pepper to taste

Method
— Preheat a browning dish
for 7 minutes at 100%;
add the butter and oil and
heat for 30 seconds at
100%.
— Sear the strips of steak,
add the onions and cook
at 100% for 3 to 4
minutes, stirring twice
during the cooking time.
Set aside.
— Dissolve the cornstarch in
the water and mix with
the beef broth; cook at
100% for 4 minutes,
stirring twice during the
cooking time.

— Add the ketchup and
sugar to the sauce and
season to taste.
— Pour the sauce over the
steak and onions and
cook at 100% for 2 to 3
minutes.
— Allow to stand for 2
minutes before serving.

Fruit Kebabs

Ingredients
1 peach, cut into quarters
1 pear, cut into quarters
1 apple, cut into quarters
1 banana, cut into thick slices
1 slice of pineapple, cut into
quarters
4 red cherries
4 green cherries
50 mL (1/4 cup) orange juice
50 mL (1/4 cup) lemon juice
50 mL (1/4 cup) honey
4 wooden skewers

Method
— In a bowl, mix the orange
juice, lemon juice and
honey. Set aside.
— Alternate the fruit on the
skewers.
— Baste the kebabs with the
sauce and suspend across
the edges of a shallow
dish.

— Cook for 2 minutes at
90% and baste again.
— Cook for 1 to 2 minutes
longer at 90%.

* To save time, prepare these dishes in
the following order; the steak and
onions, the Brussels sprouts and
parsnips and then the fruit kebabs.

Friday's Menu

Yellow Beans with Fine Herbs

Ingredients
1 540 mL (19 oz) can cut yellow beans, drained
30 mL (2 tablespoons) butter
125 mL (1/2 cup) onion, finely chopped
125 mL (1/2 cup) celery, finely chopped
15 mL (1 tablespoon) parsley, chopped
2 mL (1/2 teaspoon) basil
pinch rosemary
salt and pepper to taste

Method
— Melt the butter in a dish for 40 seconds at 100%.
— Add the onion and celery; cover and cook at 100% for 3 to 4 minutes, stirring once during the cooking time.
— Add the beans and cook for 3 to 4 minutes at 100%.
— Add the herbs and mix well.
— Season to taste before serving.

Shrimp in Cream Sauce

Ingredients
450 g (1 lb) shrimp, shelled
30 mL (2 tablespoons) butter
1 onion, chopped
1 red pepper, cut into fine strips
250 mL (1 cup) mushrooms, sliced
45 mL (3 tablespoons) cornstarch
500 mL (2 cups) 18% cream
30 mL (2 tablespoons) tomato paste
30 mL (2 tablespoons) dill or watercress, to garnish
salt and pepper to taste

Method
— Place the butter in a dish, add the onion, red pepper and mushrooms; cover and cook at 100% for 2 minutes, stirring once during the cooking time.
— Add the shrimp and cover; reduce the power to 70% and cook for 9 to 11 minutes, stirring once during the cooking time. Set aside.
— Dissolve the cornstarch in a small amount of the cream and add the tomato paste and the remaining cream.
— Cook the cream sauce at 100% for 4 minutes, until thick and smooth, stirring every minute during the cooking time.
— Add the shrimp and vegetable mixture to the sauce and heat for 2 minutes at 100%.
— Season to taste and garnish with a sprig of dill or watercress before serving.

Peach Delight

Ingredients
2 large peaches, drained and cut in half
20 mL (4 teaspoons) butter
20 mL (4 teaspoons) brown sugar
4 scoops vanilla ice cream

Method
— Place the 4 peach halves in a dish. On each half, place 5 mL (1 teaspoon) of the butter and 5 mL (1 teaspoon) of the brown sugar.
— Cook for 2 to 3 minutes at 100%, or just until the peach halves are warm.
— Serve each with a scoop of vanilla ice cream.

Saturday's Menu*

Mushroom Soup

Ingredients
250 mL (1 cup) mushrooms, thinly sliced
50 mL (1/4 cup) green onions, chopped
1 284 mL (10 oz) can cream of tomato soup
250 mL (1 cup) water
1 284 mL (10 oz) can beef consommé
2 mL (1/2 teaspoon) chervil
15 mL (1 tablespoon) parsley, chopped

Method
— Put the mushrooms and onions in a dish; cover and cook for 3 minutes at 100% and set aside.
— Mix the tomato soup with the water, add the cooked vegetables, the beef consommé and chervil and mix well.
— Cook the soup at 100% for 6 to 7 minutes, stirring once during the cooking time.
— Garnish with the parsley before serving.

Veal Escallops

Ingredients
8 veal escallops
30 mL (2 tablespoons) butter
15 mL (1 tablespoon) oil
2 leeks, whites only, chopped
1 red pepper, cut into thin strips
50 mL (1/4 cup) sherry
50 mL (1/4 cup) chicken broth
50 mL (1/4 cup) 35% cream
15 mL (1 tablespoon) marmalade
15 mL (1 tablespoon) parsley, chopped
salt and pepper to taste

Method
— Preheat a browning dish for 7 minutes at 100%; add the butter and oil and heat for 30 seconds at 100%.
— Sear the veal escallops and add the chopped leeks and the red pepper strips.
— Reduce the power to 70% and cook, covered, for 7 to 9 minutes, giving the dish a half-turn halfway through the cooking time; keep the dish covered and set aside.
— In another dish, mix the sherry, chicken broth and cream; add the marmalade and mix well; cook at 100% for 2 to 3 minutes, stirring twice during the cooking time. Season.
— Add the sauce to the veal and vegetable mixture and sprinkle with parsley before serving.

Maple Fondue

Ingredients
125 mL (1/2 cup) maple syrup
10 mL (2 teaspoons) cornstarch
500 mL (2 cups) 18% cream
2 egg yolks, lightly beaten
sponge cake, cut into cubes
an assortment of fruit, cut into chunks

Method
— Heat the maple syrup in a dish for 2 to 3 minutes at 100%; set aside.
— Dissolve the cornstarch in a small amount of the cream and set aside.
— Place the remaining cream in a bowl and heat at 100% for 4 to 5 minutes, stirring once during the cooking time.
— Add the warm cream to the syrup and set aside.
— Add the dissolved cornstarch to the egg yolks and then add this mixture to the syrup and cream, stirring constantly.
— Heat for 3 to 5 minutes at 100%, or until the mixture is thickened, beating with a whisk every minute during the cooking time.
— Serve the fondue with the sponge cake and fruit chunks; dip into the sauce with fondue forks.

* To save time, prepare the dishes in the following order: the veal escallops, the mushroom soup and then the maple fondue.

Sunday's Menu

Level of Difficulty	🍴
Preparation Time	35 min
Cost per Serving	$
Number of Servings	4
Nutritional Value	1199 calories 56.3 g protein 6.9 mg iron
Food Exchanges	6 oz meat 2 vegetable exchanges 1-1/2 fruit exchanges 5 bread exchanges 1/4 milk exchange 2 fat exchanges
Cooking Time	22 min
Standing Time	None
Power Level	100%
Write Your Cooking Time Here	

Monday's Menu

Level of Difficulty	🍴
Preparation Time	30 min
Cost per Serving	$
Number of Servings	4
Nutritional Value	891 calories 25.1 g protein 5.1 mg iron
Food Exchanges	2 oz meat 2 vegetable exchanges 2 fruit exchanges 2 bread exchanges 1 milk exchange 4 fat exchanges
Cooking Time	38 min
Standing Time	None
Power Level	100%, 70%
Write Your Cooking Time Here	

Tuesday's Menu

Level of Difficulty	
Preparation Time	30 min
Cost per Serving	$
Number of Servings	4
Nutritional Value	901 calories 47.3 g protein 7.7 mg iron
Food Exchanges	4 oz meat 4 vegetable exchanges 1 fruit exchange 1-1/2 bread exchanges 6-1/2 fat exchanges
Cooking Time	21 min
Standing Time	2 min
Power Level	100%, 70%
Write Your Cooking Time Here	

Wednesday's Menu

Level of Difficulty	
Preparation Time	25 min
Cost per Serving	$
Number of Servings	4
Nutritional Value	671 calories 54.4 g protein 5.6 mg iron
Food Exchanges	3 oz meat 3 vegetable exchanges 3 fruit exchanges 3 fat exchanges 1/2 milk exchange
Cooking Time	21 min
Standing Time	None
Power Level	100%
Write Your Cooking Time Here	

Thursday's Menu

Level of Difficulty	(utensils icon)
Preparation Time	30 min
Cost per Serving	$
Number of Servings	4
Nutritional Value	699 calories 52.3 g protein 10.7 mg iron
Food Exchanges	6 oz meat 3 vegetable exchanges 3 fruit exchanges 2-1/2 fat exchanges
Cooking Time	26 min
Standing Time	2 min
Power Level	100%, 90%
Write Your Cooking Time Here	(apple and pencil icon)

Friday's Menu

Level of Difficulty	(utensils icon)
Preparation Time	25 min
Cost per Serving	$ $
Number of Servings	4
Nutritional Value	653 calories 32 g protein 5.8 mg iron
Food Exchanges	3 oz meat 3 vegetable exchanges 1 fruit exchange 5 fat exchanges 1 milk exchange
Cooking Time	30 min
Standing Time	None
Power Level	100%, 70%
Write Your Cooking Time Here	(apple and pencil icon)

Saturday's Menu

Level of Difficulty	🍴
Preparation Time	30 min
Cost per Serving	S S
Number of Servings	4
Nutritional Value	831 calories 32.9 g protein 5.7 mg iron
Food Exchanges	3 oz meat 2 vegetable exchanges 1-1/2 fruit exchanges 2-1/4 bread exchanges 5 fat exchanges
Cooking Time	35 min
Standing Time	None
Power Level	100%, 70%
Write Your Cooking Time Here	

MICROTIPS

Foolproof Grocery Lists

As we have seen, efficient meal planning is the key to efficient cooking and the first step in such meal planning is to prepare the dinner menus for one week in advance. In planning these menus, it is important both to consider the time required to prepare and cook each meal and to choose healthy foods that will provide a well-balanced diet for your family. The menus on the preceding pages help you to achieve variety while staying within your budget.

However, all this work would be futile if at the last minute you ran out of one item or the other. It is therefore necessary to compile your shopping list with as much care as you plan your menus.

There are two quite different categories of food that you will have on your shopping list: staples, which you must always have on hand, and those specific items needed for the meals you have planned in your menus. Always list the staples as soon as they run low, without waiting to run out completely, and then determine the amounts of those ingredients specifically needed for the meals you have scheduled.

With time and practice, you will establish several sets of weekly menus, ones that can be re-used indefinitely, and a corresponding set of grocery lists, also re-useable. All you have to do is check off any missing ingredients.

Steak Southern Style

Level of Difficulty	 (fork/knife icon)
Preparation Time	10 min
Cost per Serving	$ $
Number of Servings	4
Nutritional Value	342 calories 37.5 g protein 5.7 mg iron
Food Exchanges	3.5 oz meat 1 vegetable exchange 1-1/2 fat exchanges
Cooking Time	11 to 15 min
Standing Time	None
Power Level	100%, 90%
Write Your Cooking Time Here	(apple/pencil icon)

Ingredients
4 pieces, cut from sirloin steak, slices 150 g (5 oz) each
15 mL (1 tablespoon) oil
30 mL (2 tablespoons) butter
2 cloves garlic, chopped
1 540 mL (19 oz) can tomatoes, drained and chopped
5 mL (1 teaspoon) basil
5 mL (1 teaspoon) oregano
15 mL (1 tablespoon) parsley

Method
— Place the oil, butter and garlic in a dish; heat for 2 minutes at 100%.
— Add the tomatoes and the seasonings and cook at 100% for 2 to 3 minutes, stirring once during the cooking time.
— Reduce the power to 90% and add the steaks.
— Cook to desired doneness: 5 to 6 minutes for a rare steak, 7 to 8 minutes for medium and 9 to 10 minutes for well done.

Beef Salad

Level of Difficulty	
Preparation Time	20 min
Cost per Serving	$
Number of Servings	2
Nutritional Value	267 calories 31.7 g protein 4.6 mg iron
Food Exchanges	4 oz meat 2 vegetable exchanges
Cooking Time	7 min
Standing Time	None
Power Level	100%
Write Your Cooking Time Here	

Ingredients
225 g (8 oz) roast beef, cooked and cut into strips
1 potato, cut into julienne strips
30 mL (2 tablespoons) water
1 green pepper, cut into strips
1 onion, cut into strips
115 g (4 oz) mushrooms, sliced

Vinaigrette
90 mL (3 oz) vinegar
2 mL (1/2 teaspoon) coriander
1 clove garlic, crushed
125 mL (1/2 cup) water
1 beef bouillon cube
5 mL (1 teaspoon) soy sauce
pinch marjoram
pinch oregano
pinch ginger
pepper to taste

Method
— Put the potato strips in a dish with the water; cover and cook at 100% for 3 to 5 minutes, stirring once during the cooking time; drain.
— Mix the green pepper strips, onion and mushrooms and add to the beef; add the cooked potatoes.
— Put all the ingredients for the vinaigrette into the blender and blend at high speed for a few seconds until well mixed.
— Heat the vinaigrette for 2 minutes at 100%, or until it reaches the boiling point.
— Allow the vinaigrette to cool.
— Pour the vinaigrette over the mixture of beef and vegetables and serve.

Here are the ingredients that make up this recipe, which will delight the most exacting dinner guests.

MICROTIPS

To Defrost Fruit Frozen in Plastic Bags

Measure out the desired quantity and place in a dish. Set the power at 50% and defrost the fruit in two or three cycles, stirring in between. As soon as any fruit starts to get hot, allow to stand for 5 minutes before continuing this process. 250 mL (1 cup) of fruit will take 1 to 3 minutes to defrost while 1 Litre (4 cups) will take 5 to 8 minutes.

Pork Pâté

Level of Difficulty	🍴
Preparation Time	5 min
Cost per Serving	$
Number of Servings	12 servings, 30 mL (2 tablespoons) each
Nutritional Value	138 calories 8.1 g protein 1.1 mg iron
Food Exchanges	1 oz meat 1/2 fat exchange
Cooking Time	15 min
Standing Time	None
Power Level	100%
Write Your Cooking Time Here	

Ingredients
450 g (1 lb) ground pork
125 mL (1/2 cup) cracker crumbs
1 onion, grated
250 mL (1 cup) milk
2 mL (1/2 teaspoon) cloves
2 mL (1/2 teaspoon) ginger
salt and pepper to taste

Method
— Combine all the ingredients in a dish and mix well.
— Cook at 100% for 15 minutes, stirring every 5 minutes.
— To obtain a consistency that is even smoother, put the mixture through a meat grinder.
— Refrigerate before serving.

With these ingredients you can produce a delicious pâté to serve as a spread.

MICROTIPS

Quick Homemade Soups

Soup is invariably the first course to be eliminated from the menus of people in a hurry. In the case of bouillons and other soups that require long simmering, there might well be reason to do so.

However, there are many other delicious soups requiring little preparation and cooking time that you can enjoy.

With only 250 mL (1 cup) of cooked chicken, you can make a nourishing soup for four people in less than 20 minutes. Mix the chicken with 625 mL (2-1/2 cups) hot water, 175 mL (3/4 cup) egg noodles, 125 mL (1/2 cup) frozen vegetables, 15 mL (1 tablespoon) powdered chicken concentrate and your favorite seasonings. Cook for 15 minutes at 100%. You can make a number of variations on this recipe, using leftover beef, pork or lamb (chopped or diced), cooked vegetables, legumes, rice and so on.

Let you imagination fly and you'll discover some interesting and nourishing combinations.

Sausage Meatballs

Level of Difficulty	
Preparation Time	20 min
Cost per Serving	$
Number of Servings	4
Nutritional Value	580 calories 13.3 g protein 2.6 mg iron
Food Exchanges	3.5 oz meat 1/2 fruit exchange 4 fat exchanges
Cooking Time	15 min
Standing Time	2 min
Power Level	100%, 90%
Write Your Cooking Time Here	

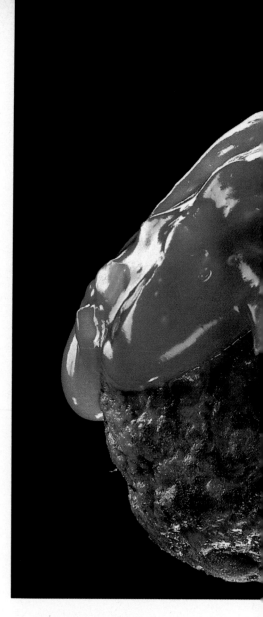

Ingredients
450 g (1 lb) sausage meat
250 mL (1 cup) pineapple chunks
30 mL (2 tablespoons) cornstarch
125 mL (1/2 cup) water
50 mL (1/4 cup) pineapple juice
50 mL (1/4 cup) brown sugar
5 mL (1 teaspoon) soy sauce
50 mL (1/4 cup) vinegar
1 small onion, grated

Method
— Form the sausage meat into meatballs and set aside.
— Drain the pineapple chunks, saving 50 mL (1/4 cup) of the juice, and set aside.
— Dissolve the cornstarch in the water and add to the pineapple juice; add the brown sugar, soy sauce and vinegar. Mix well and set aside.
— Put the onion in a dish and cook for 2 minutes at 100%; add the liquid mixture and cook for 2 minutes at 100%; stirring every minute until thickened.
— Add the meatballs and pineapple chunks to the sauce; reduce the power to 90% and cook for 9 to 11 minutes, gently stirring twice during the cooking time.
— Allow to stand for 2 minutes before serving.

As this recipe proves, a few inexpensive ingredients are enough to produce a memorable dish.

Shape the sausage meat into meatballs and set them aside.

Carefully drain the pineapple chunks, remembering to reserve the juice.

Julienne of Veal With Rice

Level of Difficulty	🍴
Preparation Time	20 min
Cost per Serving	$ $
Number of Servings	4
Nutritional Value	451 calories 35.5 g protein 5.5 mg iron
Food Exchanges	3.5 oz meat 2 vegetable exchanges 1 bread exchange 3 fat exchanges
Cooking Time	29 min
Standing Time	3 min
Power Level	100%, 90%
Write Your Cooking Time Here	

Ingredients

565 g (1-1/4 lb) veal cutlets
45 mL (3 tablespoons) butter
125 mL (1/2 cup) onion, sliced
1 green pepper, sliced
1 red pepper, sliced
250 mL (1 cup) mushrooms, sliced
30 mL (2 tablespoons) cornstarch
250 mL (1 cup) chicken broth
1 egg yolk
125 mL (1/2 cup) 35% cream
salt and pepper to taste
375 mL (1-1/2 cups) white rice, cooked

Method

— Cut the veal into thin slices and set aside.
— In a dish, melt the butter for 40 seconds at 100%; add the onion and the peppers; cover and cook at 100% for 3 to 4 minutes, stirring once during the cooking time.
— Add the mushrooms and set aside, covered.
— Dissolve the cornstarch in the broth and cook at 100% for 4 to 5 minutes, stirring every two minutes.
— Beat the egg yolk; add the cream and a small amount of the hot broth, mixing well.
— Pour the egg and cream mixture, all at once, into the broth; mix well and season to taste.
— Pour the sauce over the vegetables, add the veal slices and cook at 90% for 18 to 20 minutes, or until the veal is cooked.
— Allow to stand for 3 minutes and serve on a bed of rice.

Chicken Casserole

Level of Difficulty	(icons)
Preparation Time	20 min
Cost per Serving	$
Number of Servings	4
Nutritional Value	320 calories 32.8 g protein 2.9 mg iron
Food Exchanges	3 oz meat 2 vegetable exchanges 1 bread exchange 1/4 milk exchange
Cooking Time	16 min
Standing Time	3 min
Power Level	100%, 70%
Write Your Cooking Time Here	(icon)

Ingredients

2 whole chicken breasts, cut in half
4 carrots, thinly sliced
4 potatoes, thinly sliced
50 mL (1/4 cup) water
1 284 mL (10 oz) can cream of chicken soup
1 onion, thinly sliced
250 mL (1 cup) mushrooms, thinly sliced
2 mL (1/2 teaspoon) rosemary
pepper to taste

Method

— Put the carrots and potatoes in a casserole and add the water; cover and cook at 100% for 4 to 6 minutes, stirring halfway through the cooking time.
— While the vegetables are cooking, bone the chicken breasts and cut the meat into chunks. Set aside.
— Drain the vegetables and add the soup, onion, mushrooms and rosemary. Mix well.
— Add the chicken and season with pepper.
— Cover and cook at 70% for 8 to 10 minutes, stirring once halfway through the cooking time.
— Allow to stand for 3 minutes before serving.

Lamb Chops with Parsley

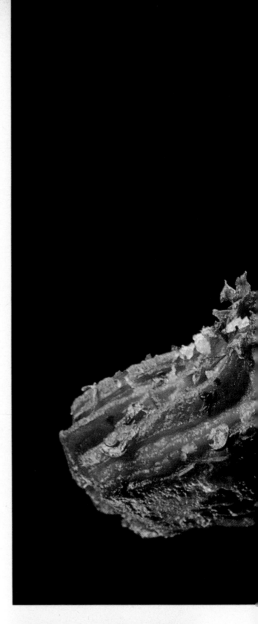

Level of Difficulty	![fork and knife icon]
Preparation Time	15 min
Cost per Serving	$ $
Number of Servings	4
Nutritional Value	338 calories 34 g protein 2.5 mg iron
Food Exchanges	3.5 oz meat 1 bread exchange 1 fat exchange
Cooking Time	10 min
Standing Time	None
Power Level	100%, 50%
Write Your Cooking Time Here	

Ingredients
8 lamb chops
375 mL (1-1/2 cups) soft breadcrumbs
50 mL (1/4 cup) dried parsley
1 clove garlic, chopped
30 mL (2 tablespoons) oil
salt and pepper to taste

Method
— Put the breadcrumbs, parsley, garlic, oil, salt and pepper into a bowl and mix well.
— Coat the chops with this mixture, pressing the coating into the meat with your hand so as to make it stick well.
— Preheat a browning dish for 7 minutes at 100% and sear the chops on both sides.
— Reduce the power to 50% and continue to cook for 9 to 10 minutes, moving the center chops to the outside and vice-versa halfway through the cooking time.

Here are the ingredients for this tasty dish: lamb chops, soft breadcrumbs, parsley, garlic, oil, salt and pepper.

Coat the chops with the mixture of all the other ingredients in the recipe. Press the coating into the meat with your hand to make sure that it sticks.

After heating the browning dish, sear the chops on both sides.

MICROTIPS

A Quick Side Dish

While the microwave oven allows you to cook vegetables very quickly, there is nothing to stop you from serving an assortment of raw vegetables. A lettuce leaf, some corn and sliced tomato would do very well and also add some color to the plate. An alternative is carrot sticks, sliced cucumber and mushrooms.

Salmon and Cheese Loaf

Level of Difficulty	
Preparation Time	10 min
Cost per Serving	**$**
Number of Servings	4
Nutritional Value	428 calories 29.2 g protein 2 mg iron
Food Exchanges	4 oz meat 1-1/2 bread exchanges 3-1/2 fat exchanges
Cooking Time	14 min
Standing Time	2 min
Power Level	70%, 50%
Write Your Cooking Time Here	

Ingredients

375 mL (1-1/2 cups) salmon, cooked
250 mL (1 cup) strong cheddar cheese, grated
1 egg, beaten
250 mL (1 cup) breadcrumbs
125 mL (1/2 cup) 10% cream
30 mL (2 tablespoons) melted butter
15 mL (1 tablespoon) lemon juice
2 mL (1/2 teaspoon) fennel
salt and pepper

Method

— Place all the ingredients in a bowl and mix well.
— Place the mixture in a loaf pan and cover the ends of the pan with strips of aluminum foil.
— Cook for 6 minutes at 70% and then remove the foil.
— Reduce the power to 50% and cook for a further 6 to 8 minutes.
— Allow to stand for 2 minutes before serving.

Assemble all the necessary ingredients to produce a dish that is delicate but distinctive.

After mixing all the ingredients, put them in a loaf pan and cover the ends of the pan with foil.

MICROTIPS

Choosing Vegetables For Blanching

Blanching is still the best way of preparing vegetables for the freezer. However, vegetables to be frozen over a long period of time should be chosen very carefully. One should choose only those that are of first quality—vegetables that are very fresh, young and tender. These essential qualities must be present to start with as freezing will preserve the existing nutritional value but can never improve on it

Cooking Times For Blanched Vegetables

Vegetables that are bought fresh and are to be frozen should be blanched to be tenderized. Cooking times will therefore be reduced to half the time normally required.

Codfish Stew

Level of Difficulty	
Preparation Time	15 min
Cost per Serving	$
Number of Servings	4
Nutritional Value	186 calories 23.7 g protein 2.3 mg iron
Food Exchanges	3 oz meat 2 vegetable exchanges
Cooking Time	19 min
Standing Time	3 min
Power Level	100%
Write Your Cooking Time Here	

Ingredients

450 g (1 lb) cod fillets
250 mL (1 cup) potatoes, cut into cubes
175 mL (3/4 cup) carrots, sliced
500 mL (2 cups) leeks, whites only, sliced
175 mL (3/4 cup) celery, chopped
125 mL (1/2 cup) onion, chopped
50 mL (1/4 cup) water
1 796 (28 oz) can tomatoes, chopped
1 bay leaf
2 mL (1/2 teaspoon)
marjoram
pinch aniseed
pinch rosemary
30 mL (2 tablespoons) parsley, chopped
30 mL (2 tablespoons) chives, chopped
salt and pepper to taste

Method

— Put the potatoes, carrots, leeks, celery and onion in a dish with the water; cover and cook at 100% for 7 to 9 minutes, stirring once during the cooking time.
— Add the tomatoes and all the seasonings; cook for 3 to 5 minutes at 100%.
— Cut the cod fillets into large cubes and add to the cooked vegetables.
— Cover and cook at 100% for 3 to 5 minutes, stirring once during the cooking time.
— Allow to stand for 3 minutes before serving.

*Healthy, tasty and nutritious
ingredients form the basis of
this remarkable dish.*

*Cut the fresh vegetables and
put them in a dish. Add the
water and cook for 7 to 9
minutes at 100%.*

Scallops with Almonds

Level of Difficulty	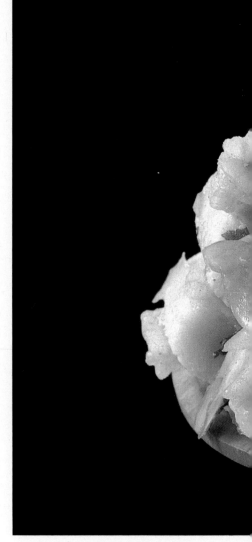
Preparation Time	10 min
Cost per Serving	$ $ $
Number of Servings	4
Nutritional Value	448 calories 25.5 g protein 4.3 mg iron
Food Exchanges	3.5 oz meat 1 bread exchange 3 fat exchanges
Cooking Time	18 min
Standing Time	None
Power Level	100%, 70%
Write Your Cooking Time Here	

Ingredients
450 g (1 lb) scallops
15 mL (1 tablespoon) oil
60 mL (4 tablespoons) butter
175 mL (3/4 cup) slivered almonds
30 mL (2 tablespoons) lemon juice
15 mL (1 tablespoon) parsley, chopped
375 mL (1-1/2 cups) curried rice, cooked
50 mL (1/4 cup) water

Method
— Preheat a browning dish for 7 minutes at 100%; add the oil and heat for 30 seconds at 100%.
— Sear the scallops.
— Reduce the power to 70%; cover and cook for 5 to 6 minutes, stirring halfway through the cooking time.
— Drain and set the scallops aside.
— Put the butter and the almonds in a dish and cook at 100% for 4 to 5 minutes, stirring twice during the cooking time.
— Add the lemon juice and parsley and mix well.
— Spoon this mixture over the scallops and set aside.
— Place the rice in a dish, add the water, cover and heat at 70% for 3 to 4 minutes, stirring once during the cooking time.
— Reheat the scallops at 70% for 2 to 3 minutes.
— Place the scallops on the hot rice and serve.

This recipe contains tasty ingredients that combine to make a harmonious union.

Sear the scallops in a preheated browning dish before cooking for 5 to 6 minutes at 70%.

Put the butter and almonds in a dish and cook at 100% for 4 to 5 minutes, stirring twice during the cooking time.

Tuna and Noodles

Level of Difficulty	🍴
Preparation Time	15 min
Cost per Serving	$
Number of Servings	4
Nutritional Value	648 calories 39.9 g protein 3.9 mg iron
Food Exchanges	3.5 oz meat 1/2 vegetable exchange 2 bread exchanges 1/2 milk exchange 2 fat exchanges
Cooking Time	17 min
Standing Time	None
Power Level	100%
Write Your Cooking Time Here	

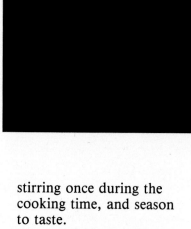

Ingredients
1 398 (14 oz) can tuna
225 g (8 oz) egg noodles
1 L (4 cups) boiling water
5 mL (1 teaspoon) salt
2 284 (10 oz) cans cream of
mushroom soup
250 mL (1 cup) milk
250 mL (1 cup) canned
mushrooms, drained
50 mL (1/4 cup) red pepper,
roasted and chopped
salt and pepper to taste
30 mL (2 tablespoons) butter
30 mL (2 tablespoons)
parsley

Method
— Put the noodles, salt and boiling water into a dish; cover and cook at 100% for 5 to 7 minutes, stirring twice during the cooking time.
— Drain the cooked noodles, rinse with cold water and set aside.
— In a dish, mix the mushroom soup and milk; cook at 100% for 4 to 5 minutes, stirring once during the cooking time.
— Add the tuna, mushrooms and red pepper; cook at 100% for 2 to 3 minutes, stirring once during the cooking time, and season to taste.
— In a small bowl, melt the butter for 30 seconds at 100% and pour over the noodles; reheat the noodles at 100% for 2 minutes, stirring once.
— Pour the tuna mixture over the noodles and sprinkle with parsley before serving.

Ham and Macaroni Casserole

Ingredients
500 mL (2 cups) ham, cut
into cubes
225 g (8 oz) long macaroni
1.5 L (6 cups) boiling water
5 mL (1 teaspoon) salt
125 mL (1/2 cup) butter
250 mL (1 cup) Parmesan
cheese, grated
salt and pepper to taste

Method
— Put the macaroni, salt,
  and boiling water in a
  dish; cover and cook at
  100% for 5 to 7 minutes,
  stirring once during the
  cooking time.
— Drain the cooked
  macaroni, rinse with cold
  water and set aside.
— Put the ham in a dish,
  heat for 3 to 4 minutes at
  100% and set aside,
  covered.

— In a small bowl, melt the
  butter at 100% for 1 to 2
  minutes, stirring once;
  pour over the macaroni.
— Sprinkle 125 mL (1/2 cup)
  of the Parmesan cheese
  over the macaroni and
  mix. Season to taste.
  Reheat the macaroni at
  100% for 2 minutes.
— Place the hot ham on the
  macaroni and sprinkle
  with the remaining
  Parmesan before serving.

Spaghettini with Eggplant

Level of Difficulty	
Preparation Time	20 min
Cost per Serving	$
Number of Servings	4
Nutritional Value	510 calories 15.6 g protein 5.3 mg iron
Food Exchanges	4 vegetable exchanges 4 bread exchanges 2 fat exchanges
Cooking Time	28 min
Standing Time	None
Power Level	100%
Write Your Cooking Time Here	

Ingredients
450 g (1 lb) spaghettini
1 L boiling water
5 mL (1 teaspoon) salt (for pasta)
1 eggplant, about 450 g (1 lb), thinly sliced
1 clove garlic, chopped
115 g (4 oz) mushrooms, thinly sliced
1 onion, chopped
30 mL (2 tablespoons) oil
170 mL (6 oz) can tomato paste
1 796 (28 oz) can Italian tomatoes, drained and chopped
30 mL (2 tablespoons) white wine
5 mL (1 teaspoon) oregano
2 mL (1/2 teaspoon) basil
2 mL (1/2 teaspoon) sugar
salt and pepper to taste

Method
— Place the eggplant, garlic, mushrooms, onion and oil in a dish; cover and cook for 3 to 4 minutes at 100%.
— Add the tomato paste, tomatoes, white wine and the seasonings; cook, uncovered, at 100% for 10 to 15 minutes, stirring every 5 minutes. Set aside.
— Put the spaghettini and the 5 mL (1 teaspoon) of salt in the boiling water and cook at 100% for 6 to 9 minutes, stirring twice during the cooking time.
— Drain the pasta and reheat the sauce.
— Pour the sauce over the spaghettini and serve.

Before starting this unusual recipe, gather all the required ingredients.

MICROTIPS

The Intelligent Use of Small Electric Appliances

When you're in a hurry, small electric appliances are useful tools in your race against time. However, they should be used judiciously. It would be pointless to dirty two beaters of a hand mixer to beat one egg, but this appliance should be used when you need to beat a large quantity of any mixture for a long time.

A knife works fine to slice, cut or chop a small quantity of food; if you are dealing with large amounts, however, it would be more efficient to use a food processor.

A blender is great for making soups but is often overlooked.

When The Munchies Strike

You've had your dinner and gone about your usual evening activities. You've never been in the habit of snacking between meals, but for the last half hour, you've had a nagging hunger that won't leave you alone and you know you can't wait until morning to satisfy it.

A little shame-faced, you search the cupboards and refrigerator for something light to satisfy those hunger pangs. You get teased about gaining weight; everyone laughs and the incident is soon forgotten.

Ten days later, the same thing happens. This time, you find a way to justify yourself. You remember the very busy day you had, even though it was quite an ordinary one. And the light dinner you ate, except that it really was quite adequate. Still, those hunger pangs attack you.

Without doubt, you're a prime candidate for attacks of the munchies!

Once you've accepted this fact, you will have to find a remedy. One should not always satisfy the munchies with sweets, potato chips and other, equally sinful, snacks.

You have a microwave oven that you've learned to use efficiently. There's not a moment to lose; the munchies have got you and you have to fight back. All you need to do is prepare some light snacks that can be cooked in your oven in a very short time. Your problem is solved. You have at your disposal a ready tool, capable of fighting the munchies whenever they attack! The recipes on the following pages offer suggestions for quick and healthy snacks that will help overcome any temptation to fill up on junk food.

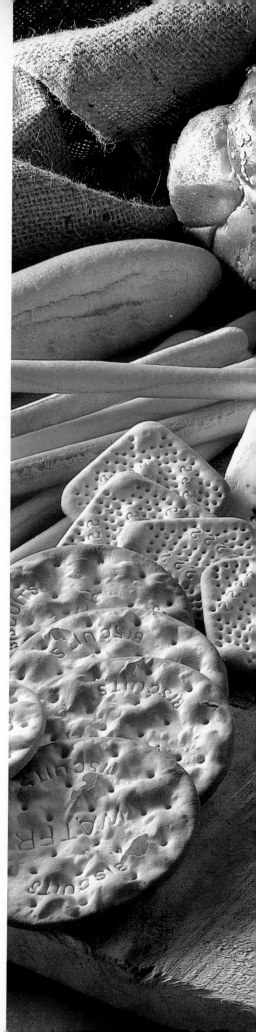

Hot Ham Sandwich

Ingredients

2 slices bread, toasted
5 mL (1 teaspoon) Dijon
mustard

2 slices ham
2 slices Emmenthal cheese
2 slices tomato
paprika to taste

Method
— Butter the slices of toast
  and spread with the
  mustard.
— On each slice place 1 slice
  of ham, 1 slice of cheese
  and 1 slice of tomato.
— Sprinkle with paprika and
  heat for 1 minute at 70%.

Level of Difficulty	🍴
Preparation Time	5 min
Cost per Serving	$
Number of Servings	2
Nutritional Value	303 calories 16.8 g protein 1.2 mg iron
Food Exchanges	2 oz meat 1 bread exchange 1-1/2 fat exchanges
Cooking Time	1 min
Standing Time	None
Power Level	70%
Write Your Cooking Time Here	🍎

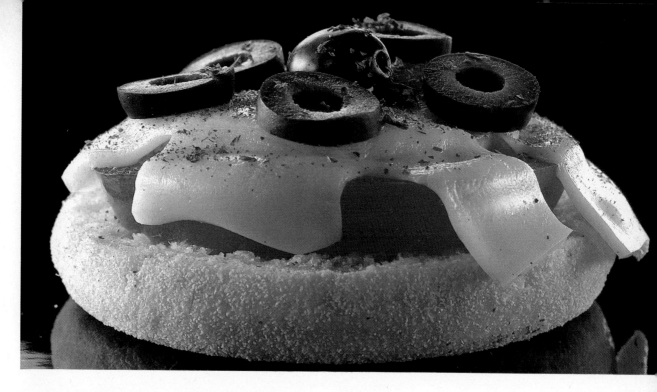

Mini Pizza Neapolitan Style

Ingredients
1 English muffin
2 thin slices onion
2 slices tomato

2 slices mozzarella cheese
4 black olives, pitted and
sliced
paprika to taste

Method
— Cut the English muffin in
half.
— Place 1 slice of onion, 1
slice of tomato, 1 slice of
mozzarella and 2 olives on
each muffin half.
— Sprinkle with paprika and
heat at 70% for 1 to 1-1/2
minutes.

Level of Difficulty	🍴
Preparation Time	5 min
Cost per Serving	$
Number of Servings	2
Nutritional Value	170 calories 10.4 g protein 1.45 mg iron
Food Exchanges	1 oz meat 1 bread exchange 1/2 fat exchange
Cooking Time	1 min 30 s
Standing Time	None
Power Level	70%
Write Your Cooking Time Here	

Mini Pizza Italian Style

Ingredients
2 slices crusty bread, toasted
8 slices pepperoni
2 slices green pepper

2 slices red pepper
2 slices Emmenthal cheese
paprika to taste

Method
— Place 4 slices of pepperoni, 1 slice of green pepper, 1 slice of red pepper and 1 slice of cheese on each slice of bread.
— Sprinkle with paprika and heat at 70% for 1-1/2 to 2 minutes.

Level of Difficulty	🍴
Preparation Time	5 min
Cost per Serving	$
Number of Servings	2
Nutritional Value	295 calories 14 g protein 0.7 mg iron
Food Exchanges	2 oz meat 1 bread exchange 1-1/2 fat exchanges
Cooking Time	2 min
Standing Time	None
Power Level	70%
Write Your Cooking Time Here	

Blanching Vegetables

Every year at harvest time, there is an abundance of fresh vegetables that are produced locally. They are available for a very short period of time and we wish the season would last longer. Too soon, the vegetables that are available are neither as fresh nor as appealing.

We can, however, preserve these vegetables at the peak of their freshness and flavor by freezing them. One word of warning though—freezing can produce excellent results or it can be a dismal failure, depending on whether or not the appropriate techniques are used. For vegetables, best results are obtained by blanching them before freezing. Blanching consists of plunging them into boiling water, cooking them briefly and then cooling them rapidly.

There are several reasons for this procedure: it lessens, to some extent, any bitterness or strong flavor in some vegetables (certain kinds of cabbage, for example); it tenderizes some of the more dense, more solid vegetables; it makes peeling easier for those vegetables that must be peeled; it preserves all the vitamins and minerals in the vegetables; and finally, it stops the action of the enzymes in vegetables, which cause them to discolor and to deteriorate. Also, vegetables that have been blanched retain their lively color and their crisp texture after they have been defrosted.

How to Blanch Vegetables

The traditional way to blanch vegetables is to immerse them in a large pot of boiling water for about half the time it would normally take to cook them. They should then be plunged immediately into a large pot of cold water with ice cubes to stop the cooking process.

You can blanch vegetables more quickly in your microwave oven by using the same method. Best results are obtained by processing 450 g (1 lb) of vegetables at a time. Use a covered casserole dish with 75 mL (1/3 cup) of water. Do not add salt or any other seasonings as these will cause the color or texture to deteriorate. Cook the vegetables in the oven at 100% power for about half the cooking time normally required for that particular vegetable. (Cooking times for many fresh vegetables are given on pages 18-19 of *Vegetables,* volume 13 of your *Microwave Magic* set). The blanching time should be divided into two or three periods so that the vegetables can be stirred once or twice.

Immediately after cooking, the vegetables should be placed in a strainer and plunged into cold water containing ice cubes until completely cooled. They are then ready to be peeled, cooked at a later time or frozen, as the case may be.

Blanching in a Freezer Bag

It is also possible to blanch vegetables in a freezer bag. Place the vegetables in the bag with the amount of water normally required to cook them and seal it. Shake the bag once or twice during the cooking. Drain the water from the freezer bag and plunge the bag into ice water until the vegetables are completely chilled. While the bag is still partially immersed in water, expel the air from it and seal it. Removing as much air as possible will greatly improve the quality of the frozen vegetables.

Pizza with Shrimp

Level of Difficulty	
Preparation Time	5 min
Cost per Serving	
Number of Servings	2
Nutritional Value	371 calories 23.8 g protein 2.2 mg iron
Food Exchanges	2 oz meat 1/2 vegetable exchange 2 bread exchanges
Cooking Time	1 min 30 s
Standing Time	None
Power Level	100%
Write Your Cooking Time Here	

MICROTIPS

Proper Freezing For Easier Defrosting

Freezing food merely to preserve it is not enough. Your freezing methods should also facilitate and speed up defrosting. Use containers that can go directly into the microwave. Divide the food you are freezing into quantities needed for one meal. You will find that defrosting and cooking will thus be greatly simplified.

Ingredients
2 small rounds of pita bread
125 mL (1/2 cup) tomato sauce
2 artichoke hearts, drained
125 mL (1/2 cup) small shrimp, cooked
2 slices mozzarella cheese
paprika to taste

Method
— Spread each round of pita bread with the tomato sauce.
— Place 1 artichoke heart and half the shrimp on each round.
— Top with a slice of mozzarella and sprinkle with paprika.
— Heat at 100% for 1 to 1-1/2 minutes.

Combined Preparation and Cooking Times for Quick Meal Recipes

All-purpose Ground Beef Base	pages 24-25	30 minutes
All-purpose Pork Base	pages 26-27	40 minutes
All-purpose Turkey Base	pages 28-29	25 minutes
Beef and Macaroni Casserole with Corn	pages 32-33	16 minutes
Beef Salad	pages 76-77	25 minutes
Chicken Casserole	pages 84-85	30 minutes
Chinese Beef Casserole	pages 34-35	20 minutes
Codfish Stew	pages 90-91	25 minutes
Curried Beef	pages 30-31	25 minutes
Ham and Macaroni Casserole	page 95	20 minutes
Hot Ham Sandwich	page 100	6 minutes
Julienne of Veal with Rice	pages 82-83	30 minutes
Lamb Chops with Parsley	pages 86-87	20 minutes
Mini Pizza Italian Style	page 102	7 minutes
Mini Pizza Neapolitan Style	page 101	7 minutes
Pita Bread Snack—Greek Style	pages 36-37	10 minutes
Pork and Onions	pages 38-39	20 minutes
Pork Pâté	pages 78-79	20 minutes
Pork with Fine Herbs	pages 42-43	25 minutes
Pork with Leeks	pages 40-41	25 minutes

Pork with Red Peppers	pages 44-45	15 minutes
Salmon and Cheese Loaf	pages 88-89	25 minutes
Sausage Meatballs	pages 80-81	30 minutes
Scallops with Almonds	pages 92-93	25 minutes
Pizza with Shrimp	page 105	7 minutes
Spaghettini with Eggplant	pages 96-97	30 minutes
Steak Southern Style	pages 74-75	15 minutes
Tuna and Noodles	page 94	25 minutes
Turkey and Cheese Casserole	pages 52-53	30 minutes
Turkey Ring	pages 46-47	20 minutes
Turkey-Stuffed Avocado	pages 50-51	20 minutes
Turkey Véronique	pages 48-49	20 minutes

This chart tabulates the average time needed for the preparation and cooking of quick meals, all-purpose meat bases and recipes using these meat bases. On page 108, you will find another chart giving the average combined times for the sample menus for one week. The cooking times given in these charts are almost always less than the simple addition of preparation and cooking times in the individual recipes would indicate because some foods would be in preparation while others are being cooked.

Combined Preparation and Cooking Times for Dinner Menus for One Week

Sunday's Menu	pages 56-57	**35 minutes**
Stuffed mushroom caps		10 minutes
Italian fondue		15 minutes
Chocolate trifle		10 minutes
Monday's Menu	pages 58-59	**38 minutes**
Cream of vegetable soup		10 minutes
Macaroni casserole		24 minutes
Apple crisp		4 minutes
Tuesday's Menu	pages 60-61	**30 minutes**
Tomatoes stuffed with avocado		10 minutes
Pork and peppers		15 minutes
Cherry caramel ring		5 minutes
Wednesday's Menu	pages 62-63	**25 minutes**
Avocado bisque		5 minutes
Chicken salad		15 minutes
Bananas with maple syrup		5 minutes
Thursday's Menu	pages 64-65	**30 minutes**
Brussels sprouts and parsnips with garlic		12 minutes
Steak and onions		15 minutes
Fruit kebabs		3 minutes
Friday's Menu	pages 66-67	**23 minutes**
Yellow Beans with Fine Herbs		5 minutes
Shrimp in cream sauce		15 minutes
Peach delight		3 minutes
Saturday's Menu	pages 68-69	**35 minutes**
Mushroom soup		8 minutes
Veal escallops		17 minutes
Maple fondue		10 minutes

Conversion Chart

**Conversion Chart for the
Main Measures Used in
Cooking**

Volume
1 teaspoon............ 5 mL
1 tablespoon........ 15 mL

1 quart (4 cups)....... 1 litre
1 pint (2 cups)....... 500 mL
1/2 cup........... 125 mL
1/4 cup............ 50 mL

Weight
2.2 lb......... 1 kg (1000 g)
1.1 lb.............. 500 g
0.5 lb.............. 225 g
0.25 lb.............. 115 g

1 oz................. 30 g

**Metric Equivalents
for Cooking
Temperatures**

49°C.............. 120°F	120°C.............. 250°F
54°C.............. 130°F	135°C.............. 275°F
60°C.............. 140°F	150°C.............. 300°F
66°C.............. 150°F	160°C.............. 325°F
71°C.............. 160°F	180°C.............. 350°F
77°C.............. 170°F	190°C.............. 375°F
82°C.............. 180°F	200°C.............. 400°F
93°C.............. 200°F	220°C.............. 425°F
107°C.............. 225°F	230°C.............. 450°F

Readers will note that, in the recipes, we give 250 mL as the
equivalent for 1 cup and 450 g as the equivalent for 1 lb and
that fractions of these measurements are even less
mathematically accurate. The reason for this is that
mathematically accurate conversions are just not practical in
cooking. Your kitchen scales are simply not accurate enough
to weigh 454 g—the true equivalent of 1 lb—and it would be
a waste of time to try. The conversions given in this series,
therefore, necessarily represent approximate equivalents, but
they will still give excellent results in the kitchen. No problems
should be encountered if you adhere to either metric or
imperial measurements throughout a recipe.

Index